JI

CATCH-22

A Dramatization

Also by
JOSEPH HELLER

CATCH–22
(Novel)

WE BOMBED IN NEW HAVEN
(Play)

CATCH-22

A Dramatization by

JOSEPH HELLER

Delacorte Press / New York

Designed by Joel Schick

Manufactured in the United States of America
First Delacorte printing

Library of Congress Cataloging in Publication Data
Heller, Joseph.
Catch–22.
1. World War, 1939–1945—Drama. I. Title.
PS3558.E476C3   812'.5'4   72–10200

CAUTION:

Professionals and amateurs are hereby warned that CATCH–22 is subject to a royalty. It is fully protected under the copyright laws of the United States of America, the British Empire, including the Dominion of Canada, and all other countries of the Copyright Union. All rights, including performance rights, whether professional, amateur, motion pictures, recitations, lecturing, public hearings, radio broadcasting, television and the rights of translation into foreign languages are strictly reserved. In its present form the play is published for the use of the reading public only.

Permission for any other use, including, without limitation, readings or performances whether by professionals or amateurs, must be obtained in writing and royalties paid. Applications for such permission and for royalty rates should be made to Samuel French Inc., 25 West 45 St., New York, N.Y. 10036, or to Robert Lantz-Candida Donadio Literary Agency, Inc., 111 West 57 St., New York, N.Y. 10019.

To
LARRY ARRICK
who labors in the theater for love,
though not always by intention.

Larry Arrick, director, with Joseph Heller, author.
John Drew Theatre, East Hampton, N. Y.
July, 1971

FOREWORD

THE first performance of *Catch–22* as a play was given at the John Drew Theater in East Hampton, New York, on July 13, 1971. It was directed by Larry Arrick, who had introduced my earlier play, *We Bombed in New Haven*, at the Yale School of Drama in 1967.

For me, for the John Drew Repertory Company, and for most of the audience and critics, the production was a success. There was praise from Alan Wallach in *Newsday* and William Raidy in the *Long Island Star* and other Newhouse newspapers, and a long and very favorable review by Mel Gussow appeared in the *New York Times*. Requests for permission to present the play began to arrive from college theater groups and other amateur and stock companies in different cities. Before the summer was over, a second production was in preparation in Chicago, by the Kingston Mines Theater Company under the direction of Gary Houston, where it played, triumphantly, I choose to assume, for twelve or sixteen weekends. There have been numerous productions since, in this country and abroad.

It was largely due to Larry Arrick that I completed the dramatization when I did. Arrick and I met again in early 1971 in connection with the videotaping of part of *We Bombed in New Haven* for National Education Television's program "The Great American Dream Machine." I remarked that I was busy with the final sections of my new novel and that in spare-time evenings I had been taking parts of *Catch-22* and attempting to transform them into some kind of dramatic form. (The motion picture was finished, and the stage and television dramatization rights had reverted to me.) Arrick disclosed that he would be directing the program for the John Drew Theater that summer and would be interested in including *Catch-22* among his productions, if there was anything of *Catch-22* to include.

Our agreement was simple. I would endeavor to hand him the first draft of a play within a month; he would produce and direct if he thought it worthwhile. At my insistence, all creative control was to be his, including the right to delete as much as he wanted to. All I had to do in return was come see the play after it had been running a few days. From his point of view, the arrangement was ideal: stage directors have learned that the most cooperative playwright is a dead one whose works are already in the public domain.

As it turned out, I had much the better of it, I feel. The play opened on a weekday to an audience, I was told by telephone, that was expectant and appreciative. The reviews in the two Long Island newspapers were laudatory. On Saturday, my wife and I, together with my nephew and his wife, drove to East Hampton from Fire Island, had a good dinner in a cozy restaurant, and enjoyed a brand-new thrilling play—*Catch-22!*—glittering (to *my* narcissistic eyes, anyway) with countless delightful staging and acting surprises I could not possibly have anticipated by keeping such distance. Most of these have been incorporated in the script. The theater was full. The audience was awake and responsive, in step with the quick tempo of the work from the start, and laughed and applauded generously; if anything, the play possibly was "too funny," a bit more humorous in that first presentation than either I or Arrick had intended or would have wished.

A few days afterward the review in the daily edition of the influential *New York Times* appeared, praising both script and production extensively and, along with Raidy and Wallach earlier, authenticating, I felt, the adaptation as a bona fide theater work, as a play with an identity of its own apart from the novel and the movie. For me, there was a happy ending to an experience that had been gratifying and comfortable throughout. (Backstage, however, an air of fatigue was present, and it was easy to detect that some members of the company were no longer on congenial terms with all of the others. They worked a schedule that summer that was unimaginably hard.)

Though the idea of finishing *Catch-22* as a play had come from Larry Arrick, the idea of starting it had been in my mind about ten years, from the time of the publication of the novel back in October, 1961: even while still writing the book I had the strong impression that many of the dialogues had a potential for effective staging, and other sections equally so if their content could be externalized competently into spoken words. This feeling was reinforced soon after publication by interest from people active in the theater. Strangers wrote, asking to be allowed to turn the novel into tragedies, comedies, and musicals, or certain chapters into one-act plays. Others did their dramatizations first and then asked permission. The book was soon a widely used source of exercise material for actors and directors working with training groups. Since so many people were already dramatizing *Catch-22*, I felt it made some sense for me to think seriously about doing it someday too. From David Merrick came a lenient and extremely liberal offer that would have let *me* try the adaptation *without* the help of a more experienced collaborator. At that time, though, I had neither the confidence nor the ambition to commit myself to a stage play. Nor did I wish to postpone the possibility of a sale of motion picture rights that would have enabled me to leave my advertising job with *McCall's* magazine.

In August of 1962, therefore, with something like a month's vacation on my hands, with no idea for a second novel in mind, and with much titillating chatter about Broadway buzzing in my ears, I began, purely as an experiment, a diversion, and a test, to take sections from the book almost at random and turn them into play-script form. At the end of August, the motion picture rights were sold, and I stopped. I reserved the stage and television dramatization rights for myself, but they were not to be used until after the release of the motion picture. By the time I stopped, I had transposed five scenes for the stage to my initial satisfaction: the trial of Clevinger, p. 76 (all page references are to the Dell paperback edition of the novel); the seizure and trial of the Chaplain by three officers who refuse to identify themselves or state their sources of authority, p. 387; the interrogation of Yossarian by two of these same three mysterious officers after he has been stabbed by Nately's whore and is lying in the hospital in need of medical attention, p. 439; a moody, intimate love scene on the beach between Yossarian and Nurse Duckett, which, in the novel, is portrayed in most general terms and contains no dialogue, pp. 345–347, 355; and the futile, desperate efforts of Doc Daneeka to establish that he is alive after an erroneous entry in a flight log places him aboard a plane that has crashed, p. 350. In the novel, the chapter about Doc Daneeka also contains almost no usable dialogue, although the progression of actions leading to his ultimate failure is stated specifically.

Already, one could diagnose in these five scenes, presumably picked with indifference, an unconscious partiality I was showing toward subjects I felt important. Four of the five are about law and repression. The other is about death.

Things have changed in the nine years since, but they have not changed much, and all but one of these scenes are included in the play. The exception is the trial of Clevinger, which was omitted for reasons of length and not of substance. By the time I went back to the play in 1971 the war in Viet Nam had been escalating openly for seven years, and the largest and most lethal belligerent in that devastating conflict was . . . us.

There is much about law in the novel. Catch–22 itself, unread, unseen, perhaps even non-existent, becomes a handy edict for overriding all safeguards to individual liberty and safety, the key element in a tricky paradigm of democratic government that allows the law to do legitimately what the law expressly prohibits itself from doing. "Catch–22 says they have a right to do anything we can't stop them from doing," the old woman in the whorehouse explains to Yossarian (p. 416), and, in practice, she is shown to be correct. Throughout the novel, there are inquisitions, trials, sneaky undercover investigations, bullying interrogations, and numerous more cruel, unpunished acts of intimidation and persecution by people in positions of power, no matter how small, against others who are decent, innocent, and harmless, or whose offenses, if committed at all, are trivial. Many of these episodes are in the play. Thematically, in fact, the play is structured around such unchecked misuses of authority in an atmosphere of war.

Much of our national experience in recent years has been characterized by the same.

Anyone in touch with the news these past few years must be aware of the many legal actions of major scope and doubtful merit that have been launched against people who have been conspicuous critics of our military actions in Indochina or active opponents of racial discrimination here at home. With heavyweight champion Muhammed Ali (Cassius Clay), who was denied conscientious objector status as a Black Muslim and subsequently found guilty in the lower courts of violating the Selective Service Act, we had an example of both. One ought to note also the many times jurors have refused to convict in these trials and the other times convictions were set aside on appeal or prosecutions discontinued — often because of illegal eavesdropping activities by law-enforcement officials. The suspicion has often been strong from the start that the true motives behind these court proceedings were not lofty but selectively spiteful: to inflict severe, disabling punishments upon these individuals more for their irreverent opposition to official policy than for actions seriously criminal. The suspicion has been substantiated by the outcomes. Legally, these cases have been fiascoes. From the vindictive point of view of the prosecution, however, they have not been entirely wasteful, for the power to put people on trial is itself the power to punish heavily. Such trials, however, are rank persecutions.

In the trial of the Black Panthers in New Haven on charges of murdering one of their members, as in the charges against Angela Davis in California in connection with the shootings outside the Marin County courthouse, people *were* killed; but in so many of the others, it has been difficult to locate a crime that took place and impossible to identify a victim who suffered by it. Where acts were committed, they were acts more of impertinence than destruction. It is doubtless true that Father Philip Berrigan, Father Daniel Berrigan, and seven other people, who all together came to be known as the Catonsville 9, poured animal blood over records in a Selective Service office in Maryland. It is difficult, however, to measure this soberly as a "crime" against the people or to believe that society has been grievously crippled as a result. Who suffered?

For want of anything more concrete, the abstract charge of conspiracy has often been lodged, that rare and heinous crime of doing nothing more than talking about doing something illicit. (What illegal conspiracies have been formed more likely originate inside the halls of justice and more likely exist in the courtroom between prosecutor, judge, and policeman, who draw their paychecks from the same bank account and depend for promotion on the same political superiors.) The public announcements at the beginning have been grandiose, and the allegations are frequently wild.

Believe it or not, in Harrisburg, Pennsylvania, recently, with John Mitchell as U.S. Attorney General, Father Philip Berrigan, who had been in prison all the while for his role in the Catonsville action, Sister Elizabeth McAllister, and four other adults, collectively known as the Harrisburg 6, were indicted and tried, at an estimated cost to the federal government of two million dollars, on charges of conspiring to kidnap Henry Kissinger, a presidential aide, as a gesture of protest against the American war in Viet Nam and, furthermore, of conspiring to blow up the underground heating system in Washington, D.C.

The charges sounded preposterous. Their credibility was not enlarged by the evidence presented in court by the federal prosecutor. (In one of those beguiling coincidences that chance constantly takes pains to provide, his name was Lynch.*) The chief witness for the government in Harrisburg was a fellow-inmate of Father Berrigan's in Lewisburg Prison, an habitual criminal working as a paid informer for the FBI for an asking price, it was revealed, of $50,000 tax free, though he received less. His testimony was unimpressive, even in Harrisburg. The jury voted ten to two for acquittal. The jurors in Harrisburg, a tranquil and conservative area selected as the site of the trial for precisely those qualities, either did not believe the government's case or did not feel that conspiring to kidnap presidential aide Henry Kissinger and hold him hostage for a week was much of a crime.

In Boston earlier, Dr. Benjamin Spock, Reverend William Coffin of Yale, author Mitchell Goodman, and Michael Ferber, a graduate student, were brought to trial for attempting to build public resistance to government operations in

* In that amusing "vicuña-coat affair" of the Eisenhower administration, the fallen official was named Adams; the businessman was Goldfine; his secretary, if memory is correct, was Paperman; and a senator with concern for the textile industry in his state was Norris Cotton.

the matter of the draft and the war. Here the charges were true. The activities and goals of the group were stated openly from the beginning and widely advertised. All went free.

As an outgrowth of the street disturbances during the National Democratic Convention in 1968, there was the trial of the Chicago 7 on very vague charges of conspiring to cross state lines for the purpose of creating those disturbances. Some of the seven were scarcely acquainted with the others if at all, and there had been no plans or communications in which all had participated. Yet, they were brought to court together, again under Attorney General John Mitchell, in a trial presided over by a distasteful old man whose crude and insulting bias soon made people stop wondering how he'd ever become a judge and start wondering how he'd ever gotten through law school. The jury acquitted the defendants of all the major charges. Because of the verdict, Black Panther leader Bobby Seale, whose case had been severed from the rest, will not be brought to trial.

Seale was acquitted also in New Haven with other Black Panthers on charges arising from the murder of one of their members. In New York City, some fifteen or so Black Panthers were tried and found not guilty of conspiring to detonate bombs in, among other places, Bloomingdale's department store. By the time of their acquittal, most had spent nearly twenty months in prison. Bail averaging about $100,000 had been set for each, an amount widely viewed as excessive for a situation in which no acts of violence had been attempted, and it would have required approximately a million and a half dollars for all to be freed during the long wait for trial. Verdicts of not guilty do not necessarily signify that Blacks get fair trials; they get fair juries—if they are lucky.

Muhammed Ali was not lucky and was found guilty. He was deprived of his heavyweight championship and he paid millions for his principles before the verdict was reversed by the U.S. Supreme Court. Active and prospering again, and brash and wise as ever, he remains perplexing to his staid peers and superiors, for in this free-enterprise culture of ours, reputable citizens are not supposed to *pay* for their principles; they are supposed to profit from them. Otherwise, what good are they?

In California now Daniel Ellsberg and Anthony Russo, Jr., are slated to go on trial someday for espionage, theft, conspiracy, and whatnot for releasing classified government documents now known as the Pentagon Papers, a voluminous effort undertaken to assemble as history the private records leading to this country's increasing involvement in the war in Indochina. One stark conclusion to be derived from the Pentagon Papers is that Lyndon Johnson and his staff cruelly and systematically lied to the press, to the American people, and to both houses of Congress about what was happening in Viet Nam and what they intended to do. (They could not lie so successfully to our "enemies" in Viet Nam, who knew the truth through experiencing it and were therefore less naïve than Congress and most of the country.)

Another utterly appalling revelation is that none of these distinguished gentlemen, these models of rectitude who were welcome in second-best homes everywhere, seemed to have experienced any compelling discomfort over playing the parts of liars in a deception about a bloody enterprise that has already produced more American dead and wounded than World War I. None resigned in disgust to denounce the others. When McGeorge Bundy left, it was for a better-paying job with the Ford Foundation.*

As to the Ellsberg trial itself, the legal possibilities, as of this date, are intriguing. The defendants were authorized to have the material; they did not steal, but photocopied, it; they did not deliver it to a foreign power but made it available to the American public through the medium of the press. A number of other copies of the entire study were in the possession of people who no longer held government position. Is *this* espionage? In the aftermath, it is clear that nothing was damaged but the reputation for efficiency and probity of a Democratic administration that was already sunk in disdain. Astonishing as it may be, rumor has it that no law exists that was broken by the release of this information. So, while Ellsberg and Russo still may go on trial in California for violating laws that might not exist, a grand jury in Boston continues hearing secret testimony on the same matter in an investigation to find some, or at least turn up somebody who is guilty of something! ("The case against Clevinger was open and shut. The only thing missing was something to charge him with." p. 73.)

Ellsberg is really being tried for *embarrassment*, for bringing confusion and ridicule to the present Nixon administration, which is not otherwise implicated by the Pentagon Papers. The charge against him and Russo is *effrontery*: as legally defined the crime of *effrontery* lies in a failure to show respect to people in high office who will never feel sure they deserve any.

---

* In this Johnson circle as well, the names are Pickwickian, although the people were not. There were Deans, a brace of Bundys, a Rusk, Walt Whitman Rostow, and Hubert Humphrey, MacNamara's band, and even two Balls, one of them good.

Catch–22 begins with a secret investigation. In the play, which is shorter, it is introduced more quickly and made more explicit. An undercover search takes place to find the person or persons guilty of writing Washington Irving's name on the envelopes of censored letters of enlisted men. Preposterous? Of course. But any more preposterous than maintaining in court with a straight face that the Harrisburg group was seriously engaged in a plot to kidnap Henry Kissinger, a presidential aide, and blow up the underground heating system of Washington, D.C.? The investigation widens, and in Act II the suspicion is voiced that the Chaplain has been concealing stolen secret documents inside a plum tomato. This is preposterous too, but hardly more improbable than the real-life event that suggested it: the Whittaker Chambers-Alger Hiss case of the 1940s in which the former produced evidence he declared had been hidden inside a pumpkin.

What all these illustrations of due process gone awry have to do with the adaptation that follows may seem somewhat remote. Reference to them, however, may help explain several of the fundamental choices made in taking subject matter from a complicated and perhaps rather long novel published ten years earlier for use in a play that must by necessity be shorter, swifter, simpler, and more direct.

It was clear from the outset that large changes would have to be made. Plays and motion pictures, unlike novels, I feel, require a distinct, prominent narrative line accelerating toward a climactic resolution that, at best, is both surprising and inevitable. Much of the book would be eliminated or compressed. Characters must be omitted or combined, and their relative importance different in the play than in the novel. The chronology was put in order. The need for unity and consolidation seemed obvious.

The first draft of the play was two hundred typewritten pages. The second, completed in time for the production in East Hampton, was down to an acceptable one hundred and thirty-one. Apart from a large number of small changes made after seeing the play performed, it is very much the same script that is published now and the one currently used in commercial and amateur productions.

Many well-known passages from the novel were excluded simply because they could not fit closely enough with what came before and what would follow. Some were discarded with joy, others abandoned reluctantly. For reasons alluded to earlier involving Reverend Coffin, both brothers Berrigan, and protest activities by other members of the clergy, I was pleased to be able to include almost in its entirety the callous arrest and trial of the Chaplain, and pleased as well to find room for the heartless insistence upon a security clearance for Yossarian before he is permitted to receive the medical care he needs. Each, in fact, helps justify the other. It was with relief that I set aside almost all of the "The Eternal City" (p. 413) and decided to omit entirely the character Orr. The former, a pivotal chapter in the novel, would, I felt, be superfluous and pedagogical in the smaller and more energetic context of the play; in addition, there would be staging problems requiring solutions that would depart egregiously from the stylistic nature of the rest. Orr, I thought, was intrinsically undramatic, for his true purposes are disguised from everyone until long after he is gone. I could have made him comical but only that, and he would have taken up space extravagantly in a narrative form in which the need for economy, I feel, is especially stringent.

The trial of Clevinger was taken out because it was too long. (As countless acting classes have discovered, the chapter "plays beautifully," and possibly I will offer it soon as a one-act play, since most of the work of dramatizing it is done.) The scene ran nearly twenty pages, too many for a secondary character whose basic function in the total organization is to come on stage as a trusting, idealistic young man and be slaughtered.

Milo Minderbinder's role is smaller; Wintergreen's larger; and Major Major and Major Danby are combined.

Milo has fewer scenes in the play, but enough to demonstrate how virtue and viciousness can exist harmoniously within one soul—if that one soul is simple and determined enough—and to epitomize the ascendance of profits over people and even patriotism. At the end, Yossarian is a fugitive, and Babbit has the bomb.

Wintergreen is unimportant as a character but indispensable as a channel of expository information necessary to make other scenes operable. He is the nucleus of the lively segment in which Doc Daneeka strives fruitlessly to convince people he is alive; I cannot think how else this passage could have been dramatized without introducing Wintergreen into it as an all-knowing mail clerk who reads everything that passes through his hand. On each of the occasions Yossarian seeks him out for help, and is, of course, refused, Wintergreen supplies the audience, through remarks to Yossarian, with details preparing the way for much larger scenes involving the Chaplain, Milo, Colonel Cathcart, Major Major, and others.

Major Major and Major Danby are compatible people in the book. Several scenes were planned for Major Major, only one for Danby—the last. I thought it better to combine them than to bring a strange character on stage for that important discussion just before the end.

There are forty parts in the play and more scenes than I have counted, to be performed by a smaller number of actors playing multiple roles. The cast at East Hampton totaled twelve, ten males and two females. Michael Lombard played such dissimilar people as the whining hypochondriac Doc Daneeka, the mocking Colonel Korn, and a nervous, frantically determined C.I.D. man zooming down like a guided missile on a startled Major Major, shifting adroitly from one part to the other with just a slight change of outer garment. Anthony Holland was a comic delight as the snarling, sexually obsessed psychiatrist and frail and touching as the Chaplain, while Adam Arkin was cast as all five young men who die. The two actresses in the cast played the eight female parts. John Pleshette played only Yossarian, and it is probably better that the person playing Yossarian do only that part.

The play is consciously cinematographic. Characters come in sight when they are ready to speak or be spoken to and leave the stage as soon as they are through, commanding attention to themselves in much the same way that a movie camera directs the gaze of an audience from one person to another. Locales change rapidly.

Both novel and play begin and end in the hospital. The war continues. The effort to "look good" supplants all other military objectives in importance. A few trifling and whimsical actions by Yossarian at the start touch off irrational investigations threatening others ceaselessly. At the end, Yossarian must choose between alternatives that are dangerous or repugnant. There is no prospect of reprieve.

"No hope," is the judgment agreed upon near the end. "No hope at all."

Minna Diskow in *Twentieth Century Literature* (Vol. 12, January, 1967, pp. 186–193) has explained more lucidly than I can how these words, which are repeated, relate to Yossarian's "Night Journey" through Rome earlier (p. 420) and how both passages can be associated with Dante's *Inferno* and that ominous warning at the entrance to Hell: "All hope abandon, ye who enter here."

Yossarian turns back in defiance, and it is with a feeling of optimism and exultation that he elects the difficult course of escape.

"At least," he says, "I'll be trying."

There've been optimistic signs in recent events that suggest such rebellious efforts at preserving one's body and one's soul may prove successful. [There is cause for pessimism too in events that are even more recent. J. H.] Outstanding among these favorable omens, I feel, are those startling, those amazing jurors, selected to the extent permissible for their built-in aversions to the defendants and the philosophies they are presumed to represent, who *refuse* to convict only because they are asked to. (I am aware that there have been countless cases receiving less attention in which atrocious penalties have been imposed for infractions that are petty or understandable. I am also aware that beyond a certain point there is no lawful remedy for these injustices perpetrated by the courts.)

There was that jury in San Jose, California, just a few weeks back that found Angela Davis *not* guilty on all counts charged! The key factors were against her: she was Black, she was educated, she was a Communist, she was militant, and she could be linked with at least one of the persons who were involved in the killings and with the weapons used. Local hostility was virulent: a white dairy farmer who advanced bail was ostracized and put out of business. But the case against her must have been lamely, despicably weak: not once in the several ballots inside the jury room was there a single vote for conviction!

When put to the test, twelve ordinary people in upper California whose names I never even bothered to note displayed more intelligence and moral sensibility in a courtroom than the prosecution gave them credit for possessing, transcended those instinctual fears and prejudices that lurk inside all of us, braved the enmity and displeasure of others in their communities, and unanimously and emphatically declared: "Not guilty!"

Bravo to them.

July 1972

CATCH-22
A Dramatization

Joseph Heller's dramatization of *Catch–22*
was first performed by The John Drew Repertory Company
at Guild Hall, East Hampton, Long Island, New York.

CAST OF CHARACTERS

JOHN PLESHETTE	Yossarian
DAVID ACKROYD	Major Major, Colonel Cathcart
ROSE ARRICK	Luciana, Patient's Mother, Nately's Mother, Old Woman, Daneeka's Mother-in-Law
JAMES BRICK	Ex-PFC Wintergreen, Nately's Father, Old Man, Investigating Major
ANTHONY HOLLAND	Chaplain, Psychiatrist
MARCIA JEAN KURTZ	Nurse Duckett, Nately's Whore, Mrs. Daneeka
MICHAEL LOMBARD	Doc Daneeka, Lieutenant Colonel Korn, C.I.D. Man
JEFFREY NIELSON	Texan, English Intern, Captain Black
LOUIS PLANTE	Milo Minderbinder, Patient's Father, Aarfy
ADAM ARKIN	Clevinger, Patient, Nately, McWatt
NEIL MOSS	Second Doctor, Corporal Whitcomb, Gus
WILLIAM REILLY	Sergeant Towser, First Doctor, Patient's Brother, Wes, Investigating Captain

Directed by Larry Arrick
Sets and lighting designed by Robert U. Taylor
Costumes designed by Patricia McGourty
Production stage manager Christopher Kelly

The Time: World War II.
The Place: An American air base off the coast of Italy.

STAGE SET

Two desks, telephones, two beds, some chairs, a table. A door frame and a window frame. A few upright coat racks. The furniture is grouped in a loose semicircle, leaving stage space on both sides and in front.

Action within the area of furniture will be action that takes place indoors. Action outside it occurs outdoors.

The doorway is used for formal entrances and exits. At other times actors move as convenient directly to where they have to go.

ACT-1

[*The* CHAPLAIN *enters carrying a pad and moves to one of the desks*]

CHAPLAIN

Dear wife. In the hospital today I met a likable young man . . .

YOSSARIAN

[*Entering*]

Me.

[YOSSARIAN *wears flight gear. He hangs his parachute harness and flight jacket on a coat rack and puts on a hospital bathrobe*]

CHAPLAIN

. . . who has a very simple wish. He wants to live forever.

YOSSARIAN

Or at least die in the attempt.

[*Lies down on bed and begins censoring letters*]

The trouble is—

[*The* TEXAN *enters, wearing pajamas and a robe, and pulls a chair up to the side of* YOSSARIAN's *bed*]

TEXAN

Hi, there. I'm from Texas. Thought I'd mosey on down the ward and get neighborly with you. What are you doing?

YOSSARIAN

Censoring letters.

TEXAN

Say, I bet *that's* exciting—reading other people's mail.

YOSSARIAN

Monotonous.

TEXAN

Ever hear of an officer here named . . . Washington?

YOSSARIAN

George?

TEXAN

Irving.

[YOSSARIAN *shakes his head*]

Ever run into a guy named . . . Irving?

YOSSARIAN

Irving what?

TEXAN

That's his last name.

[*Unhappily, as* YOSSARIAN *stares at him*]

Washington.

YOSSARIAN

Washington?

TEXAN

Irving.

[YOSSARIAN *shakes his head*]

He's been censoring letters in a most peculiar way. You're not him, are you?

YOSSARIAN

I'm Yossarian.

TEXAN

I'm mighty glad to hear that. I'll let you in on something. I'm an undercover agent, a C.I.D. man. Keep that quiet. I don't want anybody to know.

7

YOSSARIAN

Everybody knows.

TEXAN

Who told them?

YOSSARIAN

You told them. You tell everyone. Why don't you censor letters like the rest of us if you don't want anybody to suspect?

TEXAN

It's too monotonous. I'd much rather sit here and talk important topics with you. Would you like to know what I think about the republic?

[YOSSARIAN *leaves the bed with a weary groan and hangs up his bathrobe*]

I think that people of means . . . decent folk . . . should be given more votes than indecent folk . . . people without means. Don't you? It stands to reason that . . .

[*The* TEXAN *exits talking as* YOSSARIAN *retreats from him toward the* CHAPLAIN, *who rises to walk with him*]

CHAPLAIN

The Texan turned out to be good-natured, generous, and likable.

YOSSARIAN

In three minutes I couldn't stand him. He drove me out.

8

It's still going on, isn't it? Men go mad—and are rewarded with medals. And when I try to warn them, *they* think *I'm* crazy. Even Clevinger . . .

[CLEVINGER *enters and goes to the table*]

. . . who you'd think would know better, says . . .

CLEVINGER

[*Shouting*]

You're crazy!

[YOSSARIAN *spins around and joins* CLEVINGER *at the table as the* CHAPLAIN *continues offstage*]

YOSSARIAN

They're trying to kill me.

CLEVINGER

No one's trying to kill you.

YOSSARIAN

Then why are they shooting at me?

CLEVINGER

They're shooting at everyone. They're trying to kill everyone.

YOSSARIAN

And what difference does that make? Clevinger, as far back as I can remember, somebody has always been hatching a plot that will kill me. And do you know why?

CLEVINGER

Because you're crazy.

YOSSARIAN

Because I'm Assyrian.

CLEVINGER

See? You *are* crazy. There are no Assyrians. The race is extinct.

YOSSARIAN

There's one left—me. And I want very much to preserve him. Clevinger, my friend, you are one of those people with lots of intelligence . . . and no brains. In short, you are a dope.

CLEVINGER

Am I?

YOSSARIAN

Because your life is in danger—and you don't seem to care. Well, I know what to do about mine.

CLEVINGER

What?

YOSSARIAN

I'm going to see Doc Daneeka and have him take me off combat duty and send me home. He'll help.

CLEVINGER

He'll laugh in your face. He'll think you're crazy.

YOSSARIAN

Let's hope so.

[DOC DANEEKA *enters, a thermometer in his mouth, a blood-pressure apparatus on his arm*]

DOC DANEEKA

Ha . . . ha . . . ha.

[YOSSARIAN *turns back to* DOC DANEEKA *as* CLEVINGER *continues offstage*]

YOSSARIAN

What's so funny?

DOC DANEEKA

You. You're wasting your time if you expect me to help you. You must be crazy.

YOSSARIAN

Okay. Can't you ground someone who's crazy?

DOC DANEEKA

Oh, sure. There's a rule saying I *have* to ground anyone who's crazy.

YOSSARIAN

There is?

DOC DANEEKA

[*Removes thermometer*]

Sure. I don't feel so good. See? My temperature's low.

YOSSARIAN

Then why don't you ground me? I'm crazy.

DOC DANEEKA

Why don't you ask me to? Squeeze this.

YOSSARIAN

I have to ask?

DOC DANEEKA

That's what the rule says.

[*Reads blood-pressure gauge and shakes his head*]

First you have to ask. Look into my ears.

YOSSARIAN

That's all I have to do?

DOC DANEEKA

That's all. Just ask. The other ear, too.

YOSSARIAN

And then you can ground me?

DOC DANEEKA

No. Then I can't ground you. Now listen to my heart.

YOSSARIAN

You mean there's a catch?

DOC DANEEKA

Sure there's a catch. Catch-22. Anyone who wants to get out of combat duty isn't really crazy.

YOSSARIAN

Wow! I think I'm starting to get it. I'm crazy and can be grounded. All I have to do is ask, right?

DOC DANEEKA

Tap my chest. Lower.

YOSSARIAN

[*More and more rapidly*]

But as soon as I do ask, I will no longer be crazy and will have to fly more missions. I'll be *crazy* to fly more missions and sane if I don't. But if I'm sane, I have to fly them.

DOC DANEEKA

Now tap my back.

YOSSARIAN

If I fly them, I'm crazy and don't have to, but if I don't want to, I'm sane and—wowee! That's some catch, that Catch-22.

DOC DANEEKA

It's the best there is.

YOSSARIAN

Doc, you've got to help me. I'm afraid.

13

DOC DANEEKA

Of what?

YOSSARIAN

I'm afraid you're not going to help me. I get screaming night-mares. Don't you hear me?

DOC DANEEKA

I've got to laugh. I've really got to laugh when I hear you screaming your brains out every night. What about me?

YOSSARIAN

What about you?

DOC DANEEKA

What *about* me? My precious medical skills!

YOSSARIAN

What about them?

DOC DANEEKA

What *about* them? They're rusting away here, while other doctors back home are cleaning up. Do you think I enjoy hanging around here day after day refusing to help you? I wouldn't mind it so much if I could refuse to help you back in a nice plush Park Avenue office. But saying no to you here isn't easy for me, either.

YOSSARIAN

Then stop saying no. Ground me and send me home.

DOC DANEEKA

I can't. Where are you going?

[*Waving a wooden tongue depressor*]

I want to say "Aaaaah."

YOSSARIAN

To see Major Major. If my flight surgeon won't help me, my squadron commander will.

[*Exits*]

DOC DANEEKA

That's what you think! He won't even see . . .

[*Exits after* YOSSARIAN *as* MAJOR MAJOR *enters wearing a false mustache and large sunglasses, climbs through the window, and moves to a desk, taking off his disguise*]

MAJOR MAJOR

Towser!

[SERGEANT TOWSER *enters through the doorway, goes to* MAJOR MAJOR, *and salutes*]

TOWSER

Sir?

MAJOR MAJOR

Sergeant Towser. From now on I don't want anyone to come into my office to see me while I'm here. Is that clear?

TOWSER

Yes, sir. Does that include me?

MAJOR MAJOR

Yes.

TOWSER

I see. Will that be all?

MAJOR MAJOR

Yes.

TOWSER

What shall I say to people who come to see you while you are here?

MAJOR MAJOR

Tell them I'm in and ask them to wait.

TOWSER

Yes, sir. For how long?

MAJOR MAJOR

Until I've left.

TOWSER

How will you be able to leave, sir, when someone is waiting outside to see you?

MAJOR MAJOR

Through the window. From now on I'll be coming and going through the window. I don't want to see anyone anymore, and I don't want anyone to see me. Is that clear?

TOWSER

Yes, sir. And once you've left, sir, what shall I do with them?

16

MAJOR MAJOR

I don't care.

TOWSER

May I send them in to see you after you've left?

MAJOR MAJOR

Yes.

TOWSER

But you won't be here then, will you?

MAJOR MAJOR

No. That will be all.

TOWSER

Yes, sir. Will that be all?

MAJOR MAJOR

Yes. No. Tell Milo Minderbinder I won't be coming to the mess hall anymore. Tell him to have all my meals delivered to my trailer and left outside my door.

TOWSER

Yes, sir. Good-by, sir.

MAJOR MAJOR

Good-by, sergeant. And thank you. For everything.

[TOWSER *leaves.* MAJOR MAJOR *puts on his mustache and sunglasses, climbs out the window, and starts away.* YOS-

17

SARIAN *springs out of concealment and brings* MAJOR MAJOR *and himself to the ground with a pouncing tackle*]

YOSSARIAN

[*Saluting*]

Sir! Captain Yossarian requests permission to speak to the Major at once about a matter of life or death.

MAJOR MAJOR

Let me up, please. I can't return your salute while I'm lying on my arm.

[YOSSARIAN *releases him. Both men rise.* MAJOR MAJOR *returns* YOSSARIAN's *salute*]

I don't think this is the best place to talk. Go around the front and tell Sergeant Towser to send you in to see me.

YOSSARIAN

Yes, sir.

[MAJOR MAJOR *climbs back into the office through his window.* YOSSARIAN *starts around toward the doorway.* MAJOR MAJOR *counts a few seconds and then dashes suddenly back to the window and jumps out.* YOSSARIAN *comes dashing back around in time to tackle him again.*]

YOSSARIAN

[*Saluting*]

Sir! Captain Yossarian requests permission to speak to the Major at once about a matter of life or death.

MAJOR MAJOR

Permission denied.

YOSSARIAN

No, sir. That won't do.

[*Both men rise*]

MAJOR MAJOR

All right. Jump inside my office.

YOSSARIAN

After you.

[MAJOR MAJOR *climbs back inside through the window and removes his disguise.* YOSSARIAN *climbs in after him*]

MAJOR MAJOR

Well? What seems to be the trouble?

YOSSARIAN

I don't want to fly any more combat missions.

MAJOR MAJOR

Why not?

YOSSARIAN

I'm afraid.

MAJOR MAJOR

That's nothing to be ashamed of. We're all afraid.

19

YOSSARIAN

I'm not ashamed. I'm just afraid.

MAJOR MAJOR

You wouldn't be normal if you were never afraid. One of the biggest jobs we face in combat is to overcome our fear.

YOSSARIAN

Oh, come on, Major. Can't we do without that horseshit?

MAJOR MAJOR

What do you want me to tell you?

YOSSARIAN

That I've flown enough combat missions and can go home.

MAJOR MAJOR

How many have you flown?

YOSSARIAN

Fifty-one. A man was killed in my plane on the mission to Avignon.

MAJOR MAJOR

You've only got four more.

YOSSARIAN

Colonel Cathcart will raise them again. He always raises them. He wants to be a general.

MAJOR MAJOR

Perhaps he won't this time. Why don't you fly the four more missions and see what happens?

YOSSARIAN

I don't want to. I think I'd rather die than be killed.

MAJOR MAJOR

But suppose everybody on our side felt that way?

YOSSARIAN

Then I'd certainly be a damned fool to feel any other way. Wouldn't I?

MAJOR MAJOR

There's nothing I can do.

YOSSARIAN

You're a major and my squadron commander.

MAJOR MAJOR

And there's nothing I can do. Except sympathize with you secretly. I could send you to Rome.

YOSSARIAN

What for?

MAJOR MAJOR

On a rest leave. You could find a girl, get drunk, have some fun. Maybe the war will be over by the time you get back. It won't, but that's all I can do.

YOSSARIAN

It's better than nothing.

[YOSSARIAN *exits through the window and walks, while*

Rose Arrick as Luciana. John Pleshette as Yossarian.
"I'm Luciana. Why don't you pick me up?"

MAJOR MAJOR *replaces his mustache and sunglasses, climbs through the window, and leaves.* LUCIANA *enters and calls out to* YOSSARIAN *in an Italian accent*]

LUCIANA

Hey, Joe. Come here. I'm not so bad-looking.

YOSSARIAN

My name isn't Joe.

LUCIANA

I'm Luciana. Why don't you pick me up?

YOSSARIAN

My name is Yo-Yo.

LUCIANA

Okay, Joe-Joe. You picked me up. I'll go dancing with you. But I won't let you sleep with me.

YOSSARIAN

Who asked you?

[LUCIANA *pulls him to her and makes him dance with her*]

LUCIANA

You don't want to sleep with me?

YOSSARIAN

I don't want to dance with you.

LUCIANA

Okay, Joe-Joe. Then I will let you buy me dinner. But I won't let you sleep with me.

YOSSARIAN

Who asked you?

LUCIANA

You don't want to sleep with me?

YOSSARIAN

I don't want to buy you dinner.

LUCIANA

Let's go.

[*She takes his hand, pulls him to the chairs at the table. She leans back with a sigh and pats her mouth daintily*]

YOSSARIAN

You ate like a goddamn horse.

LUCIANA

Grazie. Now I feel better. Okay, Joe-Joe. Now I will let you sleep with me.

[*Pulls away in alarm as* YOSSARIAN *grabs for her*]

No—not here! Come.

[*Takes his hand and leads him to one of the beds*]

Aaaah—now.

[*They embrace.* YOSSARIAN's *attention is caught by something he feels on her back beneath her blouse*]

24

YOSSARIAN

It's long, isn't it.

LUCIANA

[*Tensing*]

Si.

YOSSARIAN

I guess this must be just about the longest and deepest scar I ever felt.

LUCIANA

It's the longest one *I* ever felt.

YOSSARIAN

Where did you get it?

LUCIANA

In an air raid.

YOSSARIAN

Germans?

LUCIANA

Americani.

YOSSARIAN

I was afraid you were going to say that. Luciana, I would like you to marry me.

LUCIANA

Tu sei pazzo.

YOSSARIAN

Why am I crazy?

LUCIANA

Perchè non posso sposare.

YOSSARIAN

Why can't you get married?

LUCIANA

Because I am not a virgin. Who will marry me?

YOSSARIAN

I will.

LUCIANA

Ma non posso sposarti.

YOSSARIAN

Why can't you marry me?

LUCIANA

Perchè sei pazzo.

YOSSARIAN

Why am I crazy?

LUCIANA

Perchè vuoi sposarmi.

YOSSARIAN

You won't marry me because I'm crazy, and you say I'm crazy because I want to marry you. Is that right?

LUCIANA

Si.

YOSSARIAN

Tu sei pazzo.

LUCIANA

Perchè? Why am I crazy?

YOSSARIAN

Because you won't marry me. *Carina, ti amo. Ti amo molto.*

LUCIANA

How can you love a girl who is not a virgin?

YOSSARIAN

It's easy. Because I can't marry you.

LUCIANA

[*Heatedly*]

Why can't you marry me? Just because I am not a virgin?

YOSSARIAN

No. Because you're crazy!

[LUCIANA *laughs and they embrace again. She rises, smooths her hair, straightens her dress*]

LUCIANA

Hey, Joe-Joe. Wake up. I have to leave now and go to work at my typewriter in my office.

27

[*Takes his hand and walks with him*]

Why don't you ask me to write my name and address on a piece of paper so that you will be able to find me again when you come to Rome?

YOSSARIAN

Why don't you write your name and address down for me on a piece of paper?

LUCIANA

[*Haughtily*]

Why? So you can tear it up into little pieces as soon as I leave?

YOSSARIAN

Who's going to tear it up?

LUCIANA

You will. And then go walking away like a big shot because a young, beautiful girl like me, Luciana, let you sleep with her and did not ask you for money.

YOSSARIAN

How much money are you asking me for?

LUCIANA

Stupido! I am not asking you for money!

[*She thrusts a slip of paper at him*]

Here, don't forget. Don't forget to tear it into tiny pieces as soon as I am gone.

[*Relenting, affectionately*]

Addio.

[*Kisses him and starts away.* YOSSARIAN *hesitates, then tears the slip of paper into tiny pieces and scatters them. He starts away jauntily in the opposite direction*]

LUCIANA
[*At the side of the stage, exiting*]

Tu sei pazzo!

[YOSSARIAN *halts abruptly. He returns to the bits of paper and stares down at them hopelessly.* WINTERGREEN *walks on stage smoking a cigar and carrying a sack labeled "U.S. Mail"*]

YOSSARIAN
Wintergreen!

WINTERGREEN
Hiyah, buddy.

YOSSARIAN
Wintergreen, I'm trying to find the name and address of a girl I met in Rome.

WINTERGREEN
Forget it. Come on inside, pal. I've got great news for you.

[WINTERGREEN *settles himself at a desk and begins sorting correspondence, writing on some papers, tearing up others.* YOSSARIAN *follows*]

I got my promotion. I'm a Pfc. now. Do you know what that means?

YOSSARIAN

You're a private first class.

WINTERGREEN

I'm an officer now, just like you. It means lots more money and prestige. I get to travel in the highest social circles now, just like you. I'm gonna go into business, compete with Milo.

YOSSARIAN

Milo won't like that.

WINTERGREEN

Good. I like to needle that bastard. Well, what can I do for you?

YOSSARIAN

Cathcart raised the number of missions again.

WINTERGREEN

I know that. I read all the mail he writes.

YOSSARIAN

Do you ever get to see any of the directives from Headquarters?

WINTERGREEN

Yo-Yo, I don't just *see* them. I print them up on my mimeograph machine and distribute them—*if* I approve. Nothing gets done without my okay. I was going to cancel the Normandy invasion, until Eisenhower committed more armor.

YOSSARIAN

How many missions am I supposed to fly?

WINTERGREEN

Forty missions is all you have to fly as far as we here at Headquarters are concerned.

YOSSARIAN

Then I can go home, right? I've got fifty-one.

WINTERGREEN

No, you can't go home. There's a catch.

YOSSARIAN

Twenty-two?

WINTERGREEN

Sure. Catch–22 says you've always got to do what your commanding officer tells you to.

YOSSARIAN

But regulations say I can go home with forty missions.

WINTERGREEN

But regulations don't say you *have* to go home. That's the catch. Even if the colonel were disobeying an order by making you fly more missions, you'd still have to fly them or you'd be guilty of disobeying an order of his. And then we would really jump on you.

YOSSARIAN

Then I really have to fly those fifty-five missions, don't I?

WINTERGREEN

Sixty. See? He's just raised them again.

YOSSARIAN

Goddamn him! What would they do to me if I refused to fly them?

WINTERGREEN

We would probably shoot you.

YOSSARIAN

We? What do you mean, *we*? Since when are you on their side?

WINTERGREEN

[*Collecting his stuff and preparing to leave*]

If you're going to be shot, whose side do you expect me to be on?

[WINTERGREEN *walks off in one direction as* MILO MINDERBINDER *enters from another, carrying a dozen eggs*]

YOSSARIAN

Milo! Have you heard the bad news?

MILO

I certainly have. Wintergreen's cutting prices.

YOSSARIAN

That's not what I meant. Colonel Cathcart just raised the missions to sixty.

MILO

Then I'm afraid you'll just have to fly them. We all have to do what we can.

YOSSARIAN

What about you?

MILO

Me? I happen to be tied down at present with my responsibilities as mess officer. I have to go to Egypt to buy cotton.

YOSSARIAN

Cotton?

MILO

Yes, I have this great chance to corner the market on Egyptian cotton. It's a big opportunity for the syndicate. And don't forget—everybody has a share.

YOSSARIAN

Do I have a share?

MILO

Everybody has a share.

Louis Plante as Milo Minderbinder. John Pleshette as Yossarian.
"I have this great chance to corner the market on
Egyptian cotton."

YOSSARIAN

[*Pleased*]

Gee, that's really something. I always wanted to own a share.

[*Sobering*]

Does Snowden own a share?

MILO

Of course. Everybody in the squadron owns a share.

YOSSARIAN

Snowden isn't in the squadron anymore. He was killed on the mission to Avignon.

MILO

That's part of his share.

YOSSARIAN

There was no morphine in the first-aid kit. There was nothing I could give him for the pain. *Just wrote that said: "What's good for Milo Minderbinder is good for the country."*

MILO

I needed the morphine to trade for these fresh eggs. You get your share, don't you?

YOSSARIAN

I don't want my share. I'm going back into the hospital.

MILO

No, Yossarian. The best thing for us to do is for you to fly your sixty missions, even if you get killed. You can't keep running into the hospital like a crybaby every time—

YOSSARIAN

Oh yes I can.

[MILO *shakes his head disapprovingly and exits as* NURSE DUCKETT *and* FIRST DOCTOR *take places at the desks inside the circle of furniture.* YOSSARIAN *moves around to the doorway and knocks. They pay no attention to him. He enters*]

Hi. Hey!

[*As they finally glance up*]

I have this sharp, persistent, throbbing pain in the lower right side of my abdomen. I think it's appendicitis.

FIRST DOCTOR

Beat it.

NURSE DUCKETT

We can't tell him to beat it. We have to keep all abdominal complaints under observation for five days because so many of them have been dying after we make them beat it.

FIRST DOCTOR

[*Leaving*]

All right, Nurse Duckett. Put him under observation for five days and *then* make him beat it. Give him an ice bag just to play safe.

[YOSSARIAN *puts on a hospital robe*]

NURSE DUCKETT

I think you're faking.

[YOSSARIAN *shrugs, moves to one of the two beds, and lies down.* NURSE DUCKETT *hands him an ice bag and leaves as* ENGLISH INTERN *enters*]

ENGLISH INTERN

Well, old boy. How is your liver?

YOSSARIAN

I think it's my appendix.

ENGLISH INTERN

[*Pressing* YOSSARIAN'*s abdomen*]

No, I'm afraid your appendix is no good, no good at all. If your appendix goes wrong, we can take it out and have you back on active duty in no time at all. But come to us with a liver complaint and you can fool us for weeks. Let's throw this silly ice bag away before you die of pneumonia. The liver, you see, is a large, ugly mystery to us. If you've ever eaten liver, you know what I mean.

YOSSARIAN

What's an English medical officer doing on duty here?

ENGLISH INTERN

[*Leaving*]

I'll tell you about that in the morning if I ever see you again. The way they whisk us around here, I never know where I'm going to—

[*Arms reach in and pull him offstage on one side as* NURSE DUCKETT *and* FIRST DOCTOR *enter from the other*]

FIRST DOCTOR

Well, good morning. Good morning, good morning, good morning. How is that sick appendix of yours?

YOSSARIAN

There's nothing wrong with my appendix. It's my liver.

NURSE DUCKETT

It was your appendix yesterday.

YOSSARIAN

It's my liver today. I ought to know.

FIRST DOCTOR

Maybe it is his liver. What does his blood count show?

NURSE DUCKETT

He hasn't had a blood count.

FIRST DOCTOR

Have one taken right away. We can't afford to take chances

with a patient in his condition. We've got to keep ourselves covered in case he dies.

[*Starting away*]

In the meantime, keep that ice bag on. It's very important.

YOSSARIAN

I don't have an ice bag.

FIRST DOCTOR

No? Well, maybe it's not so important. Just let someone know if the pain becomes unendurable.

[FIRST DOCTOR *and* NURSE DUCKETT *exit as* SECOND DOCTOR *appears*]

SECOND DOCTOR

Well, Yossarian, I'm afraid I have some very bad news for you. You're in perfect health and have to go back to combat duty. Isn't that good?

[*Leaves. Suddenly, a* PATIENT *sits up in the next bed and shouts*]

PATIENT

I see everything twice!

NURSE DUCKETT

[*Reappearing*]

What?

PATIENT

I see everything twice!

[FIRST DOCTOR *comes running back in with alarm*]

NURSE DUCKETT

He sees everything twice!

FIRST DOCTOR

What?

NURSE DUCKETT

He says he sees everything twice!

SECOND DOCTOR

Swell! Then it's *meningitis*, I'd say.

FIRST DOCTOR

Why pick meningitis? Why not, let's say, acute nephritis?

SECOND DOCTOR

Because I'm a meningitis man, that's why, and not an acute nephritis man.

FIRST DOCTOR

Well I was here first.

SECOND DOCTOR

Why don't we just roll him away into an isolation room and see what develops if he takes a turn for the worse?

FIRST DOCTOR

Suits me. There's enough of him to go around.

[*The bed is rolled off a few yards. The* DOCTORS *and* NURSE DUCKETT *start away*]

SECOND DOCTOR

[*Calling back toward* YOSSARIAN]

And get that one out of here. He's fit for duty.

YOSSARIAN

[*Sits up in bed and shouts*]

I see everything twice!

[*The* DOCTORS *and* NURSE DUCKETT *rush back to* YOSSARIAN's *bed*]

FIRST DOCTOR

Hold it! I got here first again.

SECOND DOCTOR

That's not fair.

FIRST DOCTOR

I don't care whether it's fair or not. You aren't getting this one away from me, too.

[*To* YOSSARIAN, *holding one finger up directly before him*]

How many fingers do you see?

YOSSARIAN

Two.

FIRST DOCTOR

[*Holding up two fingers*]

How many fingers do you see now?

YOSSARIAN

Two.

FIRST DOCTOR

[*Holds up none*]

And how many now?

YOSSARIAN

Two.

FIRST DOCTOR

[*Beaming*]

By Jove, he's right! He does see everything twice! Roll him away with that other one.

[YOSSARIAN's *bed is rolled beside the other bed. All but the* SECOND DOCTOR *stride away*]

PATIENT

I see everything twice!

YOSSARIAN

[*Winking at him*]

I see everything twice!

PATIENT

The walls! The walls! Move back the walls!

YOSSARIAN

The walls! The walls! Move back the walls!

[*The* PATIENT *emits a loud groan and flops back on the bed with his eyes shut.* YOSSARIAN *emits a loud groan and falls back, also. The* SECOND DOCTOR *feels the* PATIENT's *pulse, shakes his head grimly, and draws the sheet over his face*]

YOSSARIAN

What are you doing?

SECOND DOCTOR

He's dead.

YOSSARIAN

[*Sitting up in bed and shouting*]

I see everything once!

[*The* FIRST DOCTOR *and* NURSE DUCKETT *come running back*]

FIRST DOCTOR

Lemme have him.

SECOND DOCTOR

Oh, no—you had him last time. I wanna do it. So shut up now—and be a good sport.

[*Holding up one finger*]

How many fingers do you see?

YOSSARIAN

One.

SECOND DOCTOR

[*Holding up two fingers*]

How many fingers do you see now?

YOSSARIAN

One.

SECOND DOCTOR

[*Holding up ten fingers*]

And how many now?

YOSSARIAN

One.

SECOND DOCTOR

I made him all better! Oh, boy—that calls for a drink.

[*He exits with* NURSE DUCKETT, *leaving the* FIRST DOCTOR *behind*]

FIRST DOCTOR

And just in time, too. Yossarian, some relatives are here to see you. Oh, don't worry, not yours. It's the mother, father, and brother of that chap who died. They've traveled all the way from New York to see a dying soldier.

YOSSARIAN

I'm not dying.

FIRST DOCTOR

Of course you're dying. Where else do you think you're heading?

YOSSARIAN

They came to see their son.

FIRST DOCTOR

They'll have to take what they can get.

YOSSARIAN

Suppose they start crying?

FIRST DOCTOR

I'll come right in. All you've got to do is lie here a few minutes and die a little. Is that asking so much?

YOSSARIAN

All right. If it's just for a few minutes. Why don't you wrap a bandage around my head for effect?

FIRST DOCTOR

That sounds like a splendid idea.

[*He hands a molded head bandage to* YOSSARIAN, *who fits it on*]

YOSSARIAN

Why don't you get some flowers? Old ones.

FIRST DOCTOR

We haven't got time.

YOSSARIAN

At least darken the room.

FIRST DOCTOR

Shhhh!

[*He exits. A poorly dressed* OLD COUPLE *enters with a belligerent* YOUNG MAN *in a sailor's uniform. They approach timidly until they arrive at the side of the bed. They are Italian-American and reflect it in their speech*]

FATHER

He looks terrible.

BROTHER

He's sick, Pa.

MOTHER

Giuseppe.

YOSSARIAN

My name is Yossarian.

BROTHER

His name is Yossarian, Ma. Yossarian, don't you recognize me? I'm your brother John. Don't you know who I am?

YOSSARIAN

You're my brother John.

BROTHER

He does recognize me! Pa, he knows who I am. Yossarian, here's Papa. Say hello to Papa.

YOSSARIAN

Hello, Papa.

FATHER

Hello, Giuseppe.

BROTHER

His name is Yossarian, Pa.

FATHER

I can't get over how terrible he looks.

BROTHER

He's very sick, Pa. The doctor says he's going to die.

FATHER

I didn't know whether to believe the doctor or not. You know how crooked those guys are.

MOTHER

Giuseppe.

BROTHER

His name is Yossarian, Ma. She don't remember things too

good anymore. How're they treating you in here, kid? They treating you pretty good?

YOSSARIAN

Pretty good.

BROTHER

That's good. Just don't let anybody in here push you around. You're just as good as anybody else that's dying, even though you are an Italian. You've got rights, too.

[YOSSARIAN *winces and closes his eyes*]

FATHER

Now see how terrible he looks.

MOTHER

Giuseppe.

BROTHER

Ma, his name is Yossarian. Can't you remember?

YOSSARIAN

It's all right. She can call me Giuseppe if she wants to.

MOTHER

Giuseppe.

BROTHER

Don't worry, Yossarian. Everything is going to be all right.

YOSSARIAN

Don't worry, Ma. Everything is going to be all right.

48

BROTHER

Did you have a priest?

YOSSARIAN

Sure.

BROTHER

That's good. Just as long as you're getting everything you've got coming to you. We were afraid we wouldn't get here in time.

YOSSARIAN

In time for what?

BROTHER

In time to see you before you died.

YOSSARIAN

What difference would it make?

BROTHER

We didn't want you to die by yourself.

YOSSARIAN

What difference would it make?

BROTHER

He must be getting delirious. He keeps repeating the same thing over and over again.

FATHER

That's really very funny. All the time I thought his name

was Giuseppe, and now I find out his name is Yossarian. That's really very funny.

BROTHER

Ma, make him feel good. Say something to cheer him up.

MOTHER

Giuseppe.

BROTHER

It's not Giuseppe, Ma. It's Yossarian.

MOTHER

What difference does it make? He's dying.

[*She starts to cry. The* FATHER *and* BROTHER *start to cry, also*]

YOSSARIAN

What are you crying about?

MOTHER

You're dying.

[YOSSARIAN *starts crying. The* FIRST DOCTOR *enters quickly, shooting* YOSSARIAN *a dirty look*]

FIRST DOCTOR

It's time to go now.

FATHER

[*Pulling himself together*]

Giuseppe.

→ Death

make fun
of death

BROTHER

Yossarian.

FATHER

Yossarian.

YOSSARIAN

Giuseppe.

FATHER

Soon you're going to die.

[YOSSARIAN *begins to sob again*]

FIRST DOCTOR

Hey! Cut that out!

[*To the others*]

Have you any last words?

FATHER

When you talk to the man upstairs, I want you to tell Him
it ain't right for people to die when they're young. Tell Him
if they got to die at all, they got to die when they're old.
I don't think He knows it ain't right, because He's supposed
to be good, and it's been going on for a long time. Okay?

BROTHER

And don't let anybody up there push you around. You'll be

just as good as anybody else in heaven, even though you are an Italian.

MOTHER

Dress warm.

[*They exit*]

FIRST DOCTOR

Thanks, kid. You did that real well. I think we're going to have you die for us all the time.

YOSSARIAN

I think I'm going to get the hell out of here.

[YOSSARIAN *goes to the coat rack and hangs up his bathrobe. The* TEXAN *enters*]

TEXAN

Hi there, fella. I heard you were dying.

YOSSARIAN

That was somebody else.

[*The* CHAPLAIN *comes on stage, and* YOSSARIAN *moves forward to meet him*]

TEXAN

[*To himself, ominously*]

Don't be too sure.

[*Exits*]

YOSSARIAN

It's all Colonel Cathcart's fault. Why don't you do something? You're the Chaplain. You're supposed to help.

CHAPLAIN

Should I go see him? All right, I will. Even though I'm afraid of him. He's so . . .

[*They exit.*]

COLONEL CATHCART *enters wearing a black circle around one eye and an Indian headdress with several feathers. He has an empty cigarette holder in his mouth and carries a small box of tomatoes. He removes his black eye and headdress and presses a button on his desk. A deafening bell rings*]

CATHCART

Korn! Colonel Korn!

KORN

[*Dryly as he enters*]

You rang, sir?

CATHCART

Come in, Korn. I need your advice. What do you think of this cigarette holder?

KORN

It's imitation black onyx with inlaid chips of imitation ivory.

*Michael Lombard as Colonel Korn. David
Ackroyd as Colonel Cathcart.*
"With someone like General Dreedle, it could be a terrible black eye."

CATHCART

That's not what I mean. Will it help me become a general?

KORN

It might. With someone like General Dreedle, it could be a terrible black eye . . .

[CATHCART's *face falls*]

. . . while with someone like General Peckem . . .

CATHCART

It could be another feather in my cap! I think I'll take that risk. Now what about that farmhouse of mine in the hills?

KORN

A feather in your cap. But only if you use it.

CATHCART

I hate it there. I've got nothing to do. I'm not even sure where that farmhouse came from or who's paying for it. How'd I get it, anyway?

KORN

You stole it.

CATHCART

Is that legal?

KORN

Sure.

CATHCART

Well, you're the lawyer and you ought to know. How about these black-market tomatoes we're buying up and selling to Milo illegally?

KORN

That's legal, too.

CATHCART

Currency manipulation?

KORN

Legal.

CATHCART

Income-tax evasion?

KORN

That's legal, also.

CATHCART

Well, if you say so. I wish you'd gone to Harvard or Yale, though, instead of a state university. It's very degrading for someone like me to have to depend on someone like you.

KORN

I understand. That's why I try to be so helpful.

CATHCART

I appreciate that. Get the Chaplain up here. There's something I want to discuss with him.

KORN

He's already here. There's something he wants to discuss with you.

CATHCART

That's what I call a real meeting of the minds, eh? Send him in.

[KORN *exits. The* CHAPLAIN *enters*]

Come on in, Chaplain.

CHAPLAIN

Thank you, sir. Sir, I want to speak—

CATHCART

Take a look at this copy of *Life* magazine. Here's a big photograph of a colonel in England who has his chaplain say prayers in the briefing room before each mission. Do you think that prayers will work here as well as they do for these people in England?

CHAPLAIN

Yes, sir. I should think they would.

CATHCART

Then I'd like to give it a try. Maybe if we say prayers, they'll put *my* picture in *Life* magazine. What are you staring at?

CHAPLAIN

Tomatoes—I think.

CATHCART

Wanna buy some?

CHAPLAIN

No, sir. I don't think so.

CATHCART

That's all right. Milo is glad to snap up all we can produce. What was it you wanted to speak to me about?

CHAPLAIN

Sir, I—

CATHCART

We'll begin with the next mission. Now, I don't want any of this Kingdom of God or Valley of Death stuff. That's all too negative. What are you making such a face for?

CHAPLAIN

I'm sorry, sir. I happened to be thinking of the twenty-third Psalm as you said that.

CATHCART

How does that one go?

CHAPLAIN

That's the one you were just referring to, sir. "The Lord is my shepherd; I—"

CATHCART

That's the one I was just referring to. It's out. What else have you got?

58

CHAPLAIN

"Save me, O God; for the waters are come in unto—"

CATHCART

No waters. I don't like waters. Why don't we try something musical? How about the harps on the willows?

CHAPLAIN

That has the rivers of Babylon in it, sir. ". . . there we sat down, yea, we wept, when we remembered Zion."

CATHCART

Zion? Let's forget *that* one right now. I wonder how it even got in there. I'd like to keep away from the subject of religion altogether if we can.

CHAPLAIN

I'm sorry, sir. But just about all the prayers I know make at least some passing reference to God.

CATHCART

Then let's get some new ones. Why can't we take a more positive approach? Why can't we all pray for something good, like a direct hit with all our bombs? Couldn't we pray for a direct hit with all our bombs?

CHAPLAIN

Well, yes, sir, I suppose so.

CATHCART

Then that's what we'll do. It will be a feather in our cap if we pray for a direct hit with all our bombs—even if we get a direct miss. We can slip you in while we're synchronizing the watches. I don't think there's anything secret about the right time. Will a minute and a half be enough?

CHAPLAIN

Yes, sir. If it doesn't include the time necessary to excuse the atheists and admit the enlisted men.

CATHCART

What atheists? There are no atheists in my outfit. Atheism is against the law, isn't it?

CHAPLAIN

No, sir.

CATHCART

Then it's un-American, isn't it?

CHAPLAIN

I'm not sure, sir.

CATHCART

Well, I am! I'm not going to disrupt our religious services just to accommodate a bunch of lousy atheists. They can stay right where they are and pray with the rest of us. And what's all this about enlisted men? Just how the hell do they get into this act?

CHAPLAIN

I'm sorry, sir. I just assumed you would want the enlisted men to be present.

CATHCART

Well, I don't. They've got a God and a chaplain of their own, haven't they?

CHAPLAIN

No, sir.

CATHCART

You mean they pray to the same God we do?

CHAPLAIN

Yes, sir.

CATHCART

And He *listens*?

CHAPLAIN

I think so, sir.

CATHCART

Well, I'll be damned. I'd like to keep them out, anyway. Honestly, Chaplain, you wouldn't want your sister to marry an enlisted man, would you?

CHAPLAIN

My sister *is* an enlisted man.

CATHCART

Are you trying to be funny?

CHAPLAIN

Oh, no, sir. She's a master sergeant in the marines.

CATHCART

I see. Well, now that I think about it, having the men pray to God probably wasn't such a hot idea, anyway. The editors of *Life* might not cooperate.

CHAPLAIN

Will that be all, sir?

CATHCART

Yeah. Unless you've got something else to say.

CHAPLAIN

Yes, sir, I have. Sir, some of the men are very upset since you raised the number of missions to sixty. They've asked me to speak to you about it.

CATHCART

Well, you just spoke to me about it.

CHAPLAIN

They wonder why they have to keep flying more and more missions.

CATHCART

That's an administrative matter, Chaplain. Tell them it's none of their business.

CHAPLAIN

Yes, sir.

CATHCART

Help yourself to a tomato, Chaplain. Go ahead, it's on me. That's an order.

CHAPLAIN

[*Takes a tomato*]

Thank you, sir. Sir—

CATHCART

Thanks for dropping around.

CHAPLAIN

Yes, sir.

[*Bracing himself*]

Sir, I'm particularly concerned about one of the bombardiers. Captain Yossarian.

CATHCART

Who?

CHAPLAIN

Yossarian, sir. A man was killed in his plane recently and—

CATHCART

That's a funny name.

CHAPLAIN

He's in a very bad way, sir. I'm afraid he won't be able to suffer much longer without doing something desperate.

CATHCART

Is that a fact, Chaplain?

CHAPLAIN

Yes, sir. I'm afraid it is.

CATHCART

[*Ponders*]

Tell him to trust in God.

CHAPLAIN

[*Giving up*]

Thank you, sir. I will.

[CHAPLAIN *exits.* CATHCART *puts on his headdress and black eye and paces nervously*]

CATHCART

[*Wailing suddenly*]

I want to be a general!

[*Rings the clangorous bell*]

Korn! Korn!

KORN

[*Entering*]

You rang, sir?

CATHCART

We may have a problem. There is a captain named Yossarian who doesn't want to fly the sixty missions.

KORN

Yossarian? That's a funny name.

CATHCART

It's a terrible name, isn't it? There are too many esses in it, like . . .

KORN

Odious, and *insidious*.

CATHCART

Subversive. It's not one of those good, crisp, clean-cut American names like—

KORN

[*Getting it in first*]

Korn.

CATHCART

[*Eyeing him resentfully*]

Or Cathcart. I wonder how he ever got to be a captain, anyway.

KORN

You probably promoted him.

CATHCART

You probably told me to.

KORN

I probably told you not to. But you wouldn't listen.

CATHCART

I should have listened.

KORN

You never listen.

CATHCART

From now on I'll listen. Stop picking on me, will you? Maybe sixty missions are too many. Should I lower them?

KORN

Raise them. You won't impress anybody by fighting *less*.

CATHCART

A man was killed in his plane.

KORN

One man? Colonel, if we're going to start waxing sentimental about every man who might be killed . . . we might just as well not have a war.

CATHCART

Korn, you're right! I'll raise them . . . to seventy.

KORN

Put another feather in your cap.

CATHCART

It certainly won't be a black eye, will it? Here—have one for your cap. And do you know what else? I'm going to volunteer the men for Bologna.

KORN

Bologna? That's very brave of you.

CATHCART

Yes, it is. But I have confidence in my men. And I believe that no target in the world is too dangerous for *them* to attack. Tell Captain Black the good news. And let's get these damn tomatoes over to Milo. Before the Chaplain snatches another one.

[*They exit as* CAPTAIN BLACK *enters, rubbing his hands with glee*]

BLACK

Bologna? Oh, boy! Ha, ha! I can't wait to see those sons of bitches eat their liver when they find out about this one. Ha, ha, ha!

[*The* CHAPLAIN *enters, carrying his tomato. Exiting*]

Hey, Chaplain! Did you hear the good news? The men are going to Bologna. Ha, ha, ha. I can't wait to tell those bastards.

[*The* CHAPLAIN *glares disapprovingly and moves through the doorway to a desk. He clears his throat and calls out hesitantly*]

CHAPLAIN

Whitcomb! Corporal Whitcomb. Come in please.

[CORPORAL WHITCOMB *slouches onstage insolently*]

WHITCOMB

What's new?

CHAPLAIN

There's nothing new. Was anyone here to see me?

WHITCOMB

No. Just that crackpot Yossarian again.

CHAPLAIN

I'm not so sure he's a crackpot.

WHITCOMB

That's right, take his part.

[CORPORAL WHITCOMB *stamps out. He walks back in again*]

You always side with the other people. That's one of the things that's wrong with you.

CHAPLAIN

I didn't intend to side with him. I was just making a statement.

WHITCOMB

What did Colonel Cathcart want?

CHAPLAIN

Nothing important. He just wanted to discuss the idea of saying prayers in the briefing room before each mission.

WHITCOMB

All right, don't tell me.

[*He stamps out. He walks back in*]

You don't have confidence in your men. That's another one of the things that's wrong with you.

CHAPLAIN

Yes, I do. I have lots of confidence in you.

WHITCOMB

Then what about those letters?

CHAPLAIN

What letters?

WHITCOMB

How about letting me send out form letters to the next of kin of all the men we lose in combat?

CHAPLAIN

No, no. Not while I'm in charge.

WHITCOMB

Is that so? It's easy for you to sit there and shake your head while I do all the work. Didn't you see that guy from Texas outside in the purple bathrobe? That was a C.I.D. man down from the hospital on official business. He's conducting an investigation.

CHAPLAIN

I hope you're not in any trouble.

WHITCOMB

No, I'm not in any trouble. You are. They're going to crack down on you for signing Washington Irving's name to all those letters.

CHAPLAIN

What letters?

WHITCOMB

All those letters you've been signing Washington Irving's name to.

CHAPLAIN

I haven't been signing Washington Irving's name to any letters.

WHITCOMB

You don't have to lie to me. I'm not the one you have to convince.

CHAPLAIN

I'm not lying.

WHITCOMB

I don't care whether you're lying or not. A lot of that correspondence you've been tampering with is classified information.

CHAPLAIN

I haven't been tampering with any correspondence.

WHITCOMB

You don't have to lie to me. I'm not the one you have to convince.

CHAPLAIN

I'm not lying!

WHITCOMB

I don't see why you have to shout at me.

[*Walks out. Walks back in*]

That's what I get for sticking *my* neck out to warn you.

[*Walks out. Walks back in*]

I just did you the biggest favor anybody ever did you in your whole life, and you don't even know it. You don't know how to show your appreciation. That's another one of the things that's wrong with you.

CHAPLAIN

I'm sorry. I'm really very grateful to you.

WHITCOMB

Then how about letting me send out those form letters?

CHAPLAIN

No, no, no. Let's not talk about it now. Please.

WHITCOMB

I'm the best friend you've got in the whole world, and you

don't even know it. Don't you know what trouble you're in? That C.I.D. man has gone back to the hospital to write a brand-new report about that tomato.

CHAPLAIN

What tomato?

WHITCOMB

The tomato you were hiding in your hand when you showed up here. The tomato you're still hiding in your hand right this very minute!

CHAPLAIN

I'm not hiding it. I got this tomato from Colonel Cathcart.

WHITCOMB

You don't have to lie to me. I don't care whether you stole it from him or not.

CHAPLAIN

Stole it? Why should I steal a tomato from Colonel Cathcart?

WHITCOMB

That's exactly what had us both stumped. And then the C.I.D. man figured out why. He figured out that you might have some important secret papers hidden away inside it.

CHAPLAIN

In a tomato? Here, see for yourself.

WHITCOMB

Not me. I don't want it.

CHAPLAIN

Please take it. I didn't even want it.

WHITCOMB

Oh, no. Don't think you're going to stick me with it.

CHAPLAIN

I'm not trying to stick you with it.

WHITCOMB

I'm not going to forget this!

[*He stamps out. He stamps back in. He stamps back out, grinning with satisfaction once his back is to the* CHAPLAIN]

CHAPLAIN

Dear wife. There is so much unhappiness in the world, and there does not seem to be anything I can do about anybody's, not even my own. I have managed to offend Corporal Whitcomb again, and I don't know how. And now the Colonel has increased the number of missions again and volunteered the men for Bologna.

[*Exits as* YOSSARIAN, CLEVINGER, and CAPTAIN BLACK *enter*]

YOSSARIAN

[*Glumly*]

Bologna?

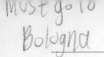
BLACK

That's right. Eat your liver, you bastards. This time you sons of bitches are really in for it. Ha, ha, ha!

[*Exits, calling offstage*]

Hey, you sons of bitches! Did you hear the good news? Ha, ha, ha.

YOSSARIAN

I don't want to go.

CLEVINGER

You have to.

YOSSARIAN

I'm going to be killed at Bologna. You're going to be killed.

CLEVINGER

We have to go, anyway.

YOSSARIAN

Are you crazy?

CLEVINGER

We're at war, Yossarian. And we have to obey orders.

YOSSARIAN

Then I'll change the orders. I've got influence. You'll see.

[*He moves inside the circle of furniture toward one of the desks*]

74

Wintergreen! Hey, Wintergreen!

[WINTERGREEN *enters with his mail sack and sits down. He begins sorting and marking letters, reading some, tearing others up*]

I need your help.

WINTERGREEN

Everybody does. I'm the most crucial figure in this whole theater of operations.

YOSSARIAN

You're only a mail clerk and a Pfc.

WINTERGREEN

Ex-Pfc. I was busted. For talking to generals by their first names. Now I'm just a poor buck private again.

YOSSARIAN

What are you doing?

WINTERGREEN

Sorting letters.

YOSSARIAN

You just tore one up.

WINTERGREEN

I didn't like it. It was too long. I like the way you censor letters when you're in the hospital. Why'd you sign Washington Irving's name to them?

YOSSARIAN

How'd you know it was me?

WINTERGREEN

I recognized the handwriting. I recognize everybody's handwriting. They've got a C.I.D. man in the hospital trying to find you.

YOSSARIAN

I know that. How'd you find out?

WINTERGREEN

I throw away all his reports. Then I throw away all the orders asking him for reports. They think he's missing in action. They've got another secret agent poking around who think's it's Major Major.

YOSSARIAN

That's funny.

WINTERGREEN

Yeah. Because Major Major *has* been signing Washington Irving's name. See? You wrote the Chaplain's name once, too, didn't you?

YOSSARIAN

For variety.

WINTERGREEN

I remember the message. "Dear Mary. I yearn for you tragically. A. C. Tappman. Group Chaplain." That really brought tears to my eyes. Say—do you want to buy some

Zippo cigarette lighters cheap? They were stolen right from quartermaster.

YOSSARIAN

Milo's selling those, too. And his aren't stolen.

WINTERGREEN

That's what *you* think. I'm selling mine for a buck apiece. What's he getting for his?

YOSSARIAN

A dollar and a penny.

WINTERGREEN

[*Laughing*]

I beat him all the time, don't I?

YOSSARIAN

He's pretty sore at you for going into competition with him.

WINTERGREEN

He's pretty sore at everyone since he cornered the market on Egyptian cotton and can't get rid of any of it. Okay, pal. Now what can I do for you?

YOSSARIAN

We have to fly to Bologna.

WINTERGREEN

Oh, I know that. I printed the orders.

YOSSARIAN

Listen—you've got a mimeograph machine, and you sort the mail. Couldn't you print up orders canceling the mission and send them out to everybody involved?

WINTERGREEN

Oh, sure. I could do that.

YOSSARIAN

What would happen?

WINTERGREEN

The mission would be canceled.

YOSSARIAN

Will you do it?

WINTERGREEN

Oh, no! I wouldn't do anything like that. There's a war on, Yossarian, and we all have our jobs to do. My job is to unload these Zippo lighters at a profit if I can. Your job is to bomb the ammunition dumps at Bologna.

YOSSARIAN

But I might be killed.

WINTERGREEN

Then you'll just have to be killed. Why can't you be a fatalist about it, the way I am? If I'm destined to unload these lighters at a profit, then that's what I'm going to do. And if you're destined to be killed over Bologna, then you're going to be killed, so you might just as well go out and die

78

like a man. Gimme a buck, will you? For the lighter. I hate to say this, Yossarian, but you're turning into a chronic complainer.

[*Exits as* CLEVINGER *comes on stage.* YOSSARIAN *moves downstage to join him*]

CLEVINGER

Wintergreen is right.

YOSSARIAN

Clevinger, you're crazy. The only reason we're going is because Cathcart volunteered us.

CLEVINGER

Unfortunately, that's none of our business.

YOSSARIAN

Do you really mean that? Do you really mean that it's none of my business how or why I get killed and that it *is* Colonel Cathcart's?

CLEVINGER

Yes, I guess I do. There are men in a better position than we are to decide how to win the war.

YOSSARIAN

Clevinger, open your eyes. It doesn't make a damned bit of difference *who* wins the war to someone who's dead.

CLEVINGER

Congratulations! I can't think of another attitude that would give greater comfort to the enemy.

YOSSARIAN

The enemy is anybody who's going to get you killed, no matter *which* side he's on. And don't you—

BLACK

[*Entering*]

Okay, boys. Let's go. It's time for Bologna.

YOSSARIAN

And don't you forget that, because the longer you remember it, the longer you might live.

CLEVINGER

I'm going to Bologna.

[CLEVINGER *takes a parachute harness from the coat rack*]

BLACK

Move it along, you bastards. Move it along.

[YOSSARIAN *hesitates, takes a parachute harness from the coat rack, and starts away with* CLEVINGER]

YOSSARIAN

Okay, okay. But I'm warning you. I'm warning you all. This is the last time I'm letting myself—

[*Exits with* CLEVINGER]

BLACK

Ha, ha, ha! Eat your liver, kid. That's what I like to see. Eat your liver.

[*The* CHAPLAIN *enters, reading aloud from his stationery pad*]

CHAPLAIN

My dear wife. Clevinger is dead.

[BLACK *takes the news with an indifferent shrug and walks out as* YOSSARIAN *returns wearily*]

YOSSARIAN

Poor bastard.

CHAPLAIN

That was the tragic flaw in all his trust and idealism, I suppose . . .

YOSSARIAN

I warned him. I told him. But . . . he wouldn't believe me, and now . . .

CHAPLAIN

. . . he is dead.

[*The* CHAPLAIN *exits with his head bowed, as* MILO *enters, carrying a box of candy, and approaches* YOSSARIAN *nervously*]

MILO

I've been looking all over for you.

YOSSARIAN

You should have looked here.

81

Louis Plante as Milo Minderbinder. John Pleshette as Yossarian.
"Chocolate-covered cotton."

cotton candy

MILO

Yossarian, I want you to help me, because you and I are friends, and that's what friends are for. Please taste this and let me know what you think. I want to serve it to the men.

YOSSARIAN

[*Taking a big bite*]

What is it?

MILO

Chocolate-covered cotton.

YOSSARIAN

[*Gagging*]

What? Take it back! Jesus Christ! You didn't even take the goddamn seeds out.

MILO

Give it a chance, will you? It can't be that bad. Is it really that bad?

YOSSARIAN

It's even worse.

MILO

But I've got to make the mess halls feed it to the men. I've got all this cotton and— *the syndicate will be ruined if they don't buy it*

[*Pointing*]

Hey! Look at that, look at that! That's the Chaplain. That's a funeral. Isn't it?

YOSSARIAN

They're burying Clevinger.

MILO

Clevinger? What happened to him?

YOSSARIAN

He got killed.

MILO

Clevinger? Oh, that's terrible. A fellow never had a better buddy than good old Clevinger. It really is terrible. And it will get even worse if the mess halls don't buy my cotton. Yossarian, what's the matter with them? Don't they understand that what's good for me is good for the country? How was I supposed to know there would be a glut? I'm still not even sure what a glut is.

YOSSARIAN

Ask Doc Daneeka.

MILO

Who ever thought the Nile Valley would be so fertile? Is it my fault I saw this wonderful opportunity to—oh, the coffin! They're lowering the coffin! I can't watch. I just can't stand here and watch those mess halls let my syndicate die. Yossarian, try eating the rest of this chocolate-covered cotton. Maybe it will taste delicious now.

YOSSARIAN

Give up, Milo. People can't eat cotton.

MILO

It isn't really cotton. It's really cotton candy, delicious cotton candy. Who will buy my delicious cotton candy? Try it and see.

YOSSARIAN

Now you're lying.

MILO

I never lie!

YOSSARIAN

You're lying now.

MILO

I only lie when it's necessary. This is better than cotton candy. It's made out of real cotton. Egyptian cotton is the finest cotton in the world.

YOSSARIAN

It's indigestible. It will make them sick. Why don't you try living on it yourself if you don't believe me?

MILO

I did.

YOSSARIAN

And?

MILO

It made me sick.

YOSSARIAN

It's all over.

MILO

It's the end. We're ruined. And all because I left them free to make their own decisions.

YOSSARIAN

Why don't you sell your cotton to the government?

MILO

The government? Oh, no. The government has no business in business. But, wait—the business of government *is* business. Calvin Coolidge said that, and Calvin Coolidge was a president, so it must be true. And the government *does* have the responsibility of buying all the Egyptian cotton I've got that no one else wants. But how will I get the government to do it?

YOSSARIAN

Bribe it.

MILO

Bribe it? Yossarian, shame on you! Bribery is against the law. But wait—it's not against the law to make a profit, is it? So it can't be against the law for me to bribe someone in order to make a fair profit, can it? But how will I know who to bribe?

YOSSARIAN

Oh, don't worry about that. Make the bribe big enough and they'll find you. Just do everything right out in the open. Don't act guilty or ashamed.

MILO

I wish you'd come with me. I won't feel safe among people who take my bribes. They're no better than a bunch of crooks.

YOSSARIAN

You'll be all right. Just tell everybody that the security of the country requires a strong domestic Egyptian cotton-speculating industry.

MILO

It does. A strong Egyptian cotton-speculating industry means a much stronger America.

YOSSARIAN

Of course it does. And point out the great number of families that depend on it for jobs and income.

MILO

A great many families do depend on it.

YOSSARIAN

You see? You're much better at it than I am. You almost make it sound true.

MILO

It *is* true.

YOSSARIAN

Now you're ready.

MILO

You're sure you won't come with me?

YOSSARIAN

You won't need me.

MILO

Good-by, Yossarian. Wish me luck. I'll never forget you for your help in this.

[*Exits. The* CHAPLAIN *returns as* YOSSARIAN *goes to the clothes rack, puts on a bathrobe, and lies down on a bed*]

CHAPLAIN

And Yossarian has gone back into the hospital.

[NURSE DUCKETT *enters to attend to* YOSSARIAN]

He says—of all things—that he has a stone in his salivary gland.

[*Exits*]

NURSE DUCKETT

I think you're faking again.

YOSSARIAN

You're very efficient.

NURSE DUCKETT

I am.

YOSSARIAN

I may be able to help you.

NURSE DUCKETT

I don't need your help.

YOSSARIAN

Who knows? Maybe . . .

[YOSSARIAN *slips his hand beneath* NURSE DUCKETT'*s skirt as she bends over and gives her a sudden touch.* NURSE DUCKETT *jumps and lets out a piercing shriek.* FIRST DOCTOR *runs in indignantly*]

FIRST DOCTOR

What happened?

YOSSARIAN

[*To* NURSE DUCKETT]

Hey, take it easy. Calm down.

FIRST DOCTOR

[*Taking* NURSE DUCKETT'*s arm*]

Is anything wrong?

[NURSE DUCKETT *screams again and pulls away from the* DOCTOR *into* YOSSARIAN'*s arms*]

YOSSARIAN

Take your filthy hands off her.

[*To* NURSE DUCKETT]

There, there. There, there, my darling. Calm down. Have a good cry if it will make you feel better. I'm not going to let him harm you.

[NURSE DUCKETT *nestles against* YOSSARIAN]

NURSE DUCKETT

Oh, thank you, thank you, darling. You're so kind . . .

YOSSARIAN

Yes.

NURSE DUCKETT

. . . so understanding.

YOSSARIAN

I know.

[*Fondling* NURSE DUCKETT]

FIRST DOCTOR

What is going *on* here?

YOSSARIAN

Nothing, sir. A little accident. I happened to have my arm out, swinging it sort of, and, well . . .

NURSE DUCKETT

[*Pleased*]

He gave me a goose.

FIRST DOCTOR

A what?

NURSE DUCKETT

A goose.

FIRST DOCTOR

A goose?

YOSSARIAN

Yeah, I guess you could call it that.

FIRST DOCTOR

How dare you give her a goose?

YOSSARIAN

I won't do it again.

NURSE DUCKETT

[*Disappointed*]

Never?

FIRST DOCTOR

You're going to be punished for this.

NURSE DUCKETT

Why?

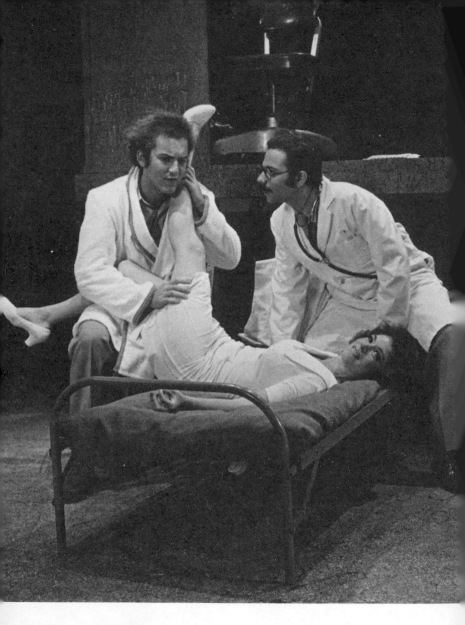

*John Pleshette as Yossarian. Marcia Jean Kurtz
as Nurse Duckett. William Reilly as First Doctor.*
"Every night I dream I'm holding a live fish in my hand."

FIRST DOCTOR

I will not permit my patients to take such liberties with the nurses in my hospital.

NURSE DUCKETT

Why not?

FIRST DOCTOR

I'm not talking to you!

YOSSARIAN

What do you want from *her*? All *she* did was scream.

NURSE DUCKETT

[*To* YOSSARIAN, *with ardent affection*]

I never knew it could be this way.

FIRST DOCTOR

Stop it! Will you let go of each other? Are you both crazy?

YOSSARIAN

Maybe *I* am. Every night I dream I'm holding a live fish in my hand.

FIRST DOCTOR

[*Coldly*]

You do *what*?

NURSE DUCKETT

He dreams he's holding a live fish in his hand.

FIRST DOCTOR

[*To* NURSE DUCKETT]

What kind of fish?

NURSE DUCKETT

Ask *him*.

FIRST DOCTOR

What kind of fish?

YOSSARIAN

I don't know. I have trouble telling one kind of fish from another.

FIRST DOCTOR

In which hand do you hold it?

YOSSARIAN

It varies.

NURSE DUCKETT

[*Helpfully*]

It probably varies with the fish.

FIRST DOCTOR

Yes? And how come *you* seem to know so much about it?

[NURSE DUCKETT *shrugs lamely*]

YOSSARIAN

She's in the dream.

FIRST DOCTOR

Well, I've got a man on my staff to listen to disgusting dreams like that. You go see Major Sanderson right now.

[*Exits as* MAJOR SANDERSON, *the psychiatrist, enters and seats himself at a desk.* YOSSARIAN *moves to him*]

PSYCHIATRIST

Come in. Come in, please. I'm Major Sanderson, your friendly staff psychiatrist. But you can call me Doctor. Just why do you think, by the way, that Colonel Ferridge finds your dream so disgusting?

YOSSARIAN

I suppose it's either some quality in the dream or some quality in Colonel Ferridge.

PSYCHIATRIST

That's very well put. For some reason Colonel Ferridge has always reminded me of a sea gull. He doesn't have much faith in psychiatry, you know.

YOSSARIAN

You don't like sea gulls, do you?

PSYCHIATRIST

No, not very much. I think your dream is charming, and I hope it recurs frequently. This fish you're holding in your hand. What does it remind you of?

YOSSARIAN

[*Pondering*]

Other fish.

Anthony Holland as Psychiatrist. John Pleshette as Yossarian.
"I think your dream is charming, and I hope it
recurs frequently."

PSYCHIATRIST

And what do other fish remind you of?

YOSSARIAN

Other fish.

PSYCHIATRIST

I'm afraid that this line of exploration is leading us nowhere. I'd like to show you some ink blots now to find out what certain shapes and colors—

YOSSARIAN

Sex.

PSYCHIATRIST

What?

YOSSARIAN

Everything reminds me of sex.

PSYCHIATRIST

Does it? Now we're *really* getting somewhere! Do you ever have any good sex dreams?

YOSSARIAN

My fish dream is a sex dream.

PSYCHIATRIST

No, I mean real sex dreams—the kind where you grab some beautiful naked bitch and rip her clothes off and throw her down to ravish her and burst into tears because you love and hate her so much you don't know what to do. *That's*

97

the kind of sex dreams I like to talk about. Don't you ever have sex dreams like that?

YOSSARIAN

[*Reflects a moment*]

That's a fish dream.

PSYCHIATRIST

[*Recoils as though slapped*]

Yes, of course. But I'd like you to dream one like that for me, anyway, just to see how you react. That will be all for today.

[YOSSARIAN *walks from the desk to* NURSE DUCKETT, *who rests on the bed comfortably, reading a magazine as she waits for him. They embrace*]

YOSSARIAN

I'm worried about Major Sanderson. He feels so rejected already. Have you got any good dreams for him?

NURSE DUCKETT

I've been having a very peculiar dream nearly all my life. I dream that I'm out swimming in water over my head and a shark is eating my left leg.

YOSSARIAN

That's a wonderful dream! I bet Major Sanderson will love it.

[YOSSARIAN *walks back to* MAJOR SANDERSON]

PSYCHIATRIST

That's a horrible dream! I'm sure you had it just to spite me. I'm not even sure you belong in the army with a disgusting dream like that.

YOSSARIAN

[*Slyly*]

Perhaps you're right, sir.

PSYCHIATRIST

Tell me, Fortiori, why—

YOSSARIAN

Who?

PSYCHIATRIST

Fortiori—why did you touch Nurse Duckett so familiarly in such an intimate place?

YOSSARIAN

I didn't do anything of the kind. I gave her a goose. That's all.

PSYCHIATRIST

All? Has it always been your habit to give gooses to—

YOSSARIAN

Geese.

PSYCHIATRIST

Yes, of course. Geese. Has it always been your habit to give geeses to all the women you meet?

YOSSARIAN

Oh, no, not all . . . but . . . well, yeah.

PSYCHIATRIST

I don't think I like you, Fortiori. I don't like your personality.

YOSSARIAN

I'm not Fortiori, sir. I'm Yossarian.

PSYCHIATRIST

Who?

YOSSARIAN

My name is Yossarian, sir.

PSYCHIATRIST

Your name is A. Fortiori! And I've got an official army record right here to prove it.

YOSSARIAN

Oh, come on, Major! I ought to know who I am.

PSYCHIATRIST

Well, you don't, and that's your problem. You've got a *split* personality, that's what I think. Yes, it's split right down the middle.

[*Grinning with cruel and insulting delight*]

I'm not saying that to be cruel and insulting. I'm not saying that because you rejected me and hurt my feelings terribly.

I'm not saying it because I hate you and want revenge. No, I'm a man of medicine, and I'm being coldly objective.

[*With enormous relish*]

Yossarian, I have very bad news for you. Are *you* man enough to take it?

YOSSARIAN

God, no! I'll go right to pieces.

PSYCHIATRIST

Can't you do even one thing right? The trouble with you is that you think you're too good for all the conventions of society. You probably think you're too good for me, too, don't you, just because I came to puberty late. Well, do you know what you are? You're a frustrated, unhappy, disillusioned, undisciplined, maladjusted young man!

YOSSARIAN

Yes, sir. I guess you're right.

PSYCHIATRIST

You're immature. You've been unable to adjust to the idea of war.

YOSSARIAN

I think that's true.

PSYCHIATRIST

You have a morbid aversion to dying.

[YOSSARIAN *nods*]

You have deep-seated survival anxieties. Subconsciously, subconsciously, there are many people you hate.

YOSSARIAN

Consciously, sir, consciously. I hate them consciously.

PSYCHIATRIST

You're antagonistic to the idea of being robbed, exploited, degraded, humiliated, or deceived. Misery depresses you.

YOSSARIAN

Yes, sir. I think that misery does.

PSYCHIATRIST

Violence depresses you. Greed depresses you. Poverty depresses you. Corruption depresses you. You know, it wouldn't surprise *me* if you're a manic-depressive.

YOSSARIAN

Yes, sir. Perhaps I am.

PSYCHIATRIST

Don't try to deny it.

YOSSARIAN

I'm not denying it, sir. I agree with everything you've said.

PSYCHIATRIST

Ah-hah! Then you admit you're crazy, do you?

YOSSARIAN

Crazy? Why is any of that crazy? You're the one who's crazy!

PSYCHIATRIST

Calling me crazy is a typically sadistic and vindictive paranoiac reaction! You really are crazy!

YOSSARIAN

Then why don't you send me home?

PSYCHIATRIST

And I'm going to send you home!

[YOSSARIAN *hurries from the desk back to* NURSE DUCKETT]

YOSSARIAN

Hey, baby, guess what! They're going to send me home!

NURSE DUCKETT

No, darling, they're not. They're sending Fortiori home because he's insane. You've been ordered back to your squadron.

YOSSARIAN

It's an outrage! I'm the one who's insane!

[*He flings off his hospital robe and charges out the doorway*]

Doc! Hey, Doc! Doc Daneeka!

[DOC DANEEKA *enters gloomily*]

DOC DANEEKA

I'm cold. I've got this chill all the time, and nobody can tell me what it is. Nobody even cares.

YOSSARIAN

Doc! Listen to me. Do you know what they just told me up at the hospital? I'm crazy. Did you know that?

DOC DANEEKA

So?

YOSSARIAN

Really crazy.

DOC DANEEKA

So?

YOSSARIAN

I'm nuts. Cuckoo. Don't you understand? I'm off my rocker. I am insane.

DOC DANEEKA

So?

YOSSARIAN

So? Don't you see what that means? Now you can take me off combat duty and send me home. They're not going to send a crazy man out to be killed, are they?

DOC DANEEKA

Who else will go?

[DANEEKA *exits.* YOSSARIAN *sits down with a pensive, sad expression.* NURSE DUCKETT *moves forward to join him*]

NURSE DUCKETT

What are you doing out here?

YOSSARIAN

Feeling sad. What a lousy earth.

NURSE DUCKETT

Cheer up, darling. Can't you?

YOSSARIAN

It's cold—a cold, cold planet. Doc Daneeka's cold, and I'm cold.

NURSE DUCKETT

We've still got a lot to be thankful for.

YOSSARIAN

Have we? You're a scatterbrain, but I love you. To whom should we be thankful? God?

NURSE DUCKETT

No, not God. You know very well I don't believe in God as much as you don't.

YOSSARIAN

Kiss me. And stop bragging. Name one thing I've got to be thankful for.

NURSE DUCKETT

Well . . . me. Aren't you thankful for me?

YOSSARIAN

Sure. But I'll bet I can name two things to be miserable about for every one you can name to be thankful for.

NURSE DUCKETT

Be thankful you're healthy.

YOSSARIAN

Be bitter you're not going to stay that way.

NURSE DUCKETT

Be glad you're alive.

YOSSARIAN

Be *furious* you're going to die.

NURSE DUCKETT

Things could be much worse.

YOSSARIAN

They could be one hell of a lot better.

NURSE DUCKETT

You're naming only one thing. You said you could name two.

YOSSARIAN

And don't tell me God works in mysterious ways. There's nothing mysterious about it. He's not working at all. He's playing.

NURSE DUCKETT

You'd better not talk that way about Him, honey. He might punish you.

YOSSARIAN

Isn't He punishing me enough? Why in the world did He ever create pain?

NURSE DUCKETT

Pain? Pain is a useful symptom. Pain is a warning to us of bodily dangers.

YOSSARIAN

And who created the dangers? Oh, He was really being charitable to us when He gave us pain. You know, we mustn't let Him get away with it—no, not the kind of God you talk about. On the Judgment Day. Yes, that's the day I'll be able to sneak close enough to grab that little yokel by His neck and—

NURSE DUCKETT

[*Hysterically*]

Stop it! Stop it!

[*She tries to beat him about the head with both fists.* YOSSARIAN *catches her wrists and restrains her gently*]

YOSSARIAN

Hey, baby, baby. Easy. What are you getting so upset about? I thought you didn't believe in God.

NURSE DUCKETT

I don't. But the God *I* don't believe in is a good God, a just God, a merciful God. Not the mean and stupid God you make Him out to be.

[YOSSARIAN *laughs and embraces her again*]

YOSSARIAN

Okay, then—let's have a little more religious freedom between us. You don't believe in the God you want to, and I won't believe in the God I want to. Is that a deal?

[*She nods, smiling through her tears, and returns his kiss*]

Thank God.

NURSE DUCKETT

I like you. Even when you're angry.

YOSSARIAN

Is that why you're trying to change me?

NURSE DUCKETT

Of course. I couldn't settle down with you the way you are. And I like you when you're sad.

YOSSARIAN

I always get sad when I stare at the sea.

NURSE DUCKETT

What are you thinking about?

YOSSARIAN

Snowden and Clevinger. Snowden froze to death in the back of my airplane. On a hot day in August. It's starting to get cold now. Do you know how many people have died under water since the world began? Neither do I. It must be millions. Sue Ann, what's going to happen to us?

NURSE DUCKETT

We're going to die.

YOSSARIAN

Must we all?

NURSE DUCKETT

That's what the doctors say.

YOSSARIAN

Then there's not much future for us, is there? Lately, I've taken to calling the roll of the dead each morning as soon as I wake up. I try to think of all the people I've ever met who are no longer alive, all the old people I knew as a child —the aunts, uncles, neighbors, parents, and grandparents, my own and everyone else's. They're all dead now. The number of dead people just keeps growing, doesn't it? I lie in my sleeping bag each morning, and that's what I think of when I wake up. Snowden, Clevinger, the roll call begins.

NURSE DUCKETT

And at night?

YOSSARIAN

I drink whiskey. And try to see you.

NURSE DUCKETT

Yo-Yo, what's going to happen to us?

YOSSARIAN

We're going to die.

NURSE DUCKETT

Am I going to marry you?

YOSSARIAN

No. I don't think you'll want to.

NURSE DUCKETT

I'm glad. My mother wouldn't like you. I'll be much better off marrying somebody happy and stable. Like a doctor. I'm beginning to miss you already.

YOSSARIAN

I used to think I was going to live forever. I was sure that by the time I grew up all you people would find a cure for everything. But now I'm all grown up, and you haven't, and I know I won't. I know I'm going to lose.

NURSE DUCKETT

Don't cry, darling.

YOSSARIAN

I'm not crying. It's that damn ocean. And the chill in the air. And the spray. I guess I am. Sue Ann, I don't want to die. I don't want to die for Colonel Cathcart.

NURSE DUCKETT

Then don't. Shhh. Be calm, darling.

[*Kissing his ear*]

I love to do this to you. Let's go inside. I love to tease you like this and set you on fire.

YOSSARIAN

I'm glad.

NURSE DUCKETT

And then I love to satisfy you. I'm so glad you let me.

YOSSARIAN

Say things like that and I will want to marry you.

NURSE DUCKETT

Yossarian, tell me truthfully. Am I the only girl you ever loved?

YOSSARIAN

No.

NURSE DUCKETT

I'm so glad.

[*Curtain*]

ACT-2

[YOSSARIAN *enters carrying a bottle of beer and an over-night bag into which he puts some toilet articles.*]

YOSSARIAN

My pal Nately is a pretty good kid. But a little crazy, too. He had a bad start—he came from a good family. Why, the poor kid had even had a very happy childhood. He got on well with all his brothers and sisters, and he did not hate his mother and father, even though they had both been very good to him.

[NATELY *comes onstage with his* FATHER *and* MOTHER. NATELY *wears his uniform and carries a small overnight bag*]

FATHER

Son, always remember that your mother is a Daughter of the American Revolution.

MOTHER

And your father is a son of a bitch.

FATHER

You are not a Vanderbilt . . .

MOTHER

. . . whose fortune was made by a vulgar tugboat captain, or a Rockefeller . . .

FATHER

. . . whose wealth was amassed through unscrupulous speculations in *crude* petroleum. You are a Nately.

MOTHER

And we Natelys have never done *anything* for our money.

FATHER

It is my wish that you join the Air Corps, where you can train safely as a pilot while the war ends.

MOTHER

As an officer you will associate only with gentlemen and frequent only the very best places.

[NATELY, *nodding constantly, shakes hands with his* FATHER, *kisses his* MOTHER, *and walks from them through the doorway to join* YOSSARIAN]

NATELY

I'm back! I got my pass. Where is she? Darling—I'm here!

YOSSARIAN

Working, probably.

NATELY

Don't say that about her.

YOSSARIAN

Don't ask me about her. It's not my fault you fell in love with a whore.

[NATELY'S WHORE *enters in skirt and slip and embraces him warmly*]

NATELY'S WHORE

Hey, *caro*! *Caro mio*. I miss you so much.

[*The* OLD MAN *and the* OLD WOMAN *drift in, smiling at the lovers*]

NATELY

Get dressed.

NATELY'S WHORE

[*Puzzled*]

Perchè?

NATELY

Why? Because I don't want other men to see you without all your clothes on.

NATELY'S WHORE

Perchè no?

NATELY

Perchè no? Because it isn't right, that's why.

NATELY'S WHORE

Why not?

NATELY

Why not? Because I say so! I'm the man, and you have to do what I say. From now on I forbid you to leave your room unless you have all your clothes on.

NATELY'S WHORE

Are you crazy? *Tu sei pazzo!*

[*She begins to stamp offstage*]

NATELY

And I don't want you ever to talk to me that way.

NATELY'S WHORE

No? *Tu sei pazzo! Idiota! Tu sei un pazzo imbecille!*

[*Exits*]

NATELY

[*To* OLD WOMAN]

From now on I want you to watch her all the time and see that she behaves properly.

OLD WOMAN

Lui è pazzo? .

YOSSARIAN

Si. He is stark, raving *pazzo.*

NATELY

[*To* YOSSARIAN]

From now on I don't want you to look at her unless she's fully dressed.

YOSSARIAN

Then make her keep her clothes on.

NATELY

She doesn't listen to me. So from now on maybe you ought to stop hanging around here.

YOSSARIAN

Why should I? It's my whorehouse.

NATELY

Then look in another direction when she comes in that way. Please?

[NATELY'S WHORE *returns, buttoning her blouse*]

NATELY'S WHORE

Marrone!

OLD WOMAN

Marrone!

NATELY

[*To* OLD MAN]

You, too. I don't want you to hang around here, either.

OLD MAN

It's my house.

NATELY

Marrone!

YOSSARIAN

The next thing you know, you'll try to make her give up hustling.

NATELY

[*To* WHORE]

From now on I forbid you to be a prostitute anymore.

NATELY'S WHORE

Perchè?

NATELY

Perchè? It's not nice, that's why! I'll give you all the money you need.

NATELY'S WHORE

And what will I do all day instead?

NATELY

What all your friends do.

NATELY'S WHORE

My friends are all prostitutes.

118

NATELY

Then get new friends! Prostitution is bad! Everybody knows that, even him.

[*Turning to the* OLD MAN]

Right?

OLD MAN

Wrong. It provides fresh air and lots of wholesome exercise.

NATELY

From now on I never want you to speak with this wicked old man.

NATELY'S WHORE

Va fongul! What does he want from me? If you think my friends are so bad, tell your friends not to come here and ficky-fick all the time with my friends!

NATELY

[*To* YOSSARIAN]

From now on I think you and the other fellows ought to stop shacking up with her friends and settle down and get married, too.

YOSSARIAN

Va fongul!

OLD MAN

He's crazy.

NATELY'S WHORE

What's the matter with you?

OLD WOMAN

È pazzo. That's what's the matter with him.

NATELY'S WHORE

Si. È pazzo. Now that you made me get dressed, I'm going to bed.

NATELY

What's the matter with everyone? Are you all crazy?

NATELY'S WHORE

Are you coming?

YOSSARIAN

I'm going. So long, kid. Have a nice leave.

[*Exits*]

NATELY

Why doesn't anybody listen to me?

OLD MAN

Why should we? You are so brave, and pure, and silly. You should try to be more like me.

NATELY

You? You're immoral!

OLD MAN

Of course.

120

NATELY

Don't you have any principles?

OLD MAN

Not many.

NATELY

Any patriotism?

OLD MAN

Not really.

NATELY

You should be ashamed! You're cynical, selfish, and un-scrupulous.

OLD MAN

I am also a hundred and seven years old. I see you don't believe that, either.

NATELY

I don't believe anything you say.

OLD MAN

It's a pity. Because they are going to kill you if you don't watch out. How old are you? Twenty-five? Twenty-six?

NATELY

Nineteen. I'll be twenty in three weeks.

OLD MAN

If you live.

NATELY'S WHORE

[*Reappearing*]

Hey, Nately! Come to bed.

OLD MAN

Go. Make love.

NATELY

That's a highly personal matter between me and her.

OLD MAN

All right. Go attend to your highly personal matter. And I will look the other way and pretend you are performing a very patriotic service.

[NATELY *exits with* WHORE]

OLD WOMAN

È pazzo?

OLD MAN

[*Shrugging sadly*]

Si. È pazzo.

[*They leave.* YOSSARIAN *reappears on stage, looking grim and moves through doorway*]

YOSSARIAN

Hey!

[OLD WOMAN *enters*]

Not you. Nately's whore.

[NATELY'S WHORE *enters*]

I've got bad news for you. It's Nately. He's dead. A midair collision. We were coming off the target after this stupid mission to—

NATELY'S WHORE
[*Lashing at his face*]

Bruto!

[YOSSARIAN *fights to restrain her*]

Bruto! Bruto!

YOSSARIAN
[*Flinging her away*]

What do you want from me?

[NATELY'S WHORE *seizes a letter opener from one of the desks and rushes at him*]

NATELY'S WHORE
Assassino!

[YOSSARIAN *twists the letter opener from her hand*]

YOSSARIAN

Stop! Listen to me, will you?

[NATELY'S WHORE *dives for the letter opener.* YOSSARIAN *disarms her again and throws the letter opener out the window. She seizes a pair of scissors and attacks again. Enter the* OLD MAN]

OLD WOMAN

Nately. Dead.

YOSSARIAN

[*Twists the scissors from her grasp*]

But I didn't do it.

[*To* NATELY'S WHORE]

Now calm down. Please. That's better. Now you're being reasonable.

[NATELY'S WHORE *kicks him in the groin.* YOSSARIAN *doubles over with a loud, quavering moan.* NATELY'S WHORE *mauls him with both fists and rushes out*]

YOSSARIAN

Dumb bitch! Why is she blaming me? Go talk to her, will you? I think she'll listen now. Try to get her—

[NATELY'S WHORE *returns with a long bread knife and goes for* YOSSARIAN'S *back*]

124

YOSSARIAN

Oh, no!

[YOSSARIAN *struggles with her and knocks the knife from her hand*]

Goddamn you! What do you want from *me*?

[*They fall to the bed,* YOSSARIAN *on top of her, grappling. She begins embracing him*]

NATELY'S WHORE

Ooooh, *caro.*

YOSSARIAN

There, there. That's better. There, there.

NATELY'S WHORE

Kiss me. *Caro mio.* Ooooh. Kiss me again.

[YOSSARIAN *responds to her embraces. As one of her hands caresses and excites him, the other gropes for the knife*]

YOSSARIAN

That's good now. There, there. Should we be doing this?

NATELY'S WHORE

Si.

YOSSARIAN

Is it right, that you and I should be . . .

125

NATELY'S WHORE

[*Raising the knife to plunge it into his back*]

Si! It's right.

[YOSSARIAN *turns in time. He wrests the knife from her and hurls it away. She begins to weep*]

YOSSARIAN

[*Consoling her*]

Please. There, there, that's right—have a good cry if it will make you feel better. There, there.

NATELY'S WHORE

[*Meekly*]

Grazie. Grazie.

[*She sniffles. He gives her his handkerchief. She dries her tears*]

Grazie. Grazie.

[*She claws viciously at his eyes*]

Ha! *Assassino!*

[YOSSARIAN, *half blinded, flings her from him. She goes for the knife. He gets it first and hurls it away. He moves toward the door*]

YOSSARIAN

'm getting the hell out of here.

[*He makes a menacing fist as she starts after him. She collapses in tears against the* OLD MAN]

I was only trying to help.

OLD MAN

You go now—with your help.

[YOSSARIAN *bolts out the door. He hurries around the circle of furniture. As he passes the window,* NATELY'S WHORE *stabs at him with another knife. He jumps out of the way and continues walking. The* CHAPLAIN *comes onstage to join him*]

YOSSARIAN

Why was she blaming me? I didn't kill him.

CHAPLAIN

We didn't save him, either.

YOSSARIAN

I went all the way to Rome to do her a favor. I was going to give her money and help her get settled.

CHAPLAIN

Are you sure you didn't imagine the whole thing?

YOSSARIAN

Huh?

[NATELY'S WHORE, *wearing a black eye, a false mustache and military fatigues, comes tiptoeing up behind* YOSSARIAN *with a long knife raised to stab him*]

CHAPLAIN

That you didn't just imagine that Nately's girl friend tried to kill you?

[YOSSARIAN *whirls around in time as* NATELY'S WHORE *lunges at him with the knife*]

NATELY'S WHORE

Caramba!

[*They struggle.* YOSSARIAN *takes away the knife and pushes her to the* CHAPLAIN]

YOSSARIAN

Hold her! Don't let her go!

[*Running out*]

McWatt! McWatt!

NATELY'S WHORE

Let me go. Please. Hey, handsome. I'll give you all the ficky-fick you want if you let me kill him.

CHAPLAIN

Oh, no! Please. I'm a happily married man.

NATELY'S WHORE

kay. I give you ficky-fick first.

[*She embraces the* CHAPLAIN. *Embarrassed, he loosens his grip. She starts away. He grabs her back. She caresses him again. His dilemma is excruciating. He releases her just as* YOSSARIAN *hurries back with* MCWATT. YOSSARIAN *grabs the tablecloth from the table and throws it over her head*]

YOSSARIAN

McWatt! Here, I got her. Hold her. Do it for me, will you?

McWATT

Oh, well. What the hell . . .

[YOSSARIAN *pushes* NATELY'S WHORE *and* MCWATT *off-stage and returns alone*]

YOSSARIAN

Whew!

CHAPLAIN

What are you doing with her?

YOSSARIAN

McWatt will fly her back to Rome and dump her at the airport. Boy, am I glad to be rid of her!

CHAPLAIN

As I started to say—

YOSSARIAN

I wonder how she got here.

[*Whirls around at an imaginary noise*]

Maybe she'll find her way back.

CHAPLAIN

Maybe you're imagining the whole thing.

YOSSARIAN

What?

CHAPLAIN

That she tried to kill you.

YOSSARIAN

Imagining it? You were right here, weren't you? She just tried it again.

CHAPLAIN

Maybe I'm imagining it, too.

YOSSARIAN

Maybe you're only imagining that you're imagining it.

[*Exits*]

CHAPLAIN

Dear wife. I think I am under a strain. I keep imagining that everything that happens has happened before and is going to happen again unless someone stands up and does

130

omething that will stop everything that has happened from
appening again. And now my assistant, Corporal Whit-
omb, has been promoted to sergeant.

[WHITCOMB *enters, getting into a shirt with sergeant's
stripes*]

Not by me, of course. If it were up to me—

WHITCOMB

Colonel Cathcart wants to see you. Right away. You never
should have stolen that plum tomato.

CHAPLAIN

I didn't steal any plum tomato.

WHITCOMB

I'm not the one you have to convince. He wants to see you
about the letters.

CHAPLAIN

What letters?

WHITCOMB

You never should have signed Washington Irving's name to
those letters.

CHAPLAIN

I didn't sign Washington Irving's name to any letters!

WHITCOMB

Not those letters. He wants to see you about the form
letters I want to send home to the families of casualties.

CHAPLAIN

Those? How did he find out about them?

WHITCOMB

I went to his office and told him.

CHAPLAIN

You did *what*? Corporal Whitcomb, do—

WHITCOMB

Sergeant. It's *Sergeant* Whitcomb now.

CHAPLAIN

Do you mean to tell me that you went over my head to the Colonel without asking my permission?

WHITCOMB

Yep. I sure did. And he promoted me to sergeant. Him and me are pretty good friends now, so you better watch out. You know something? That dumb bastard really thinks it's one of the best ideas he's ever heard.

[*As* WHITCOMB *leaves in one direction,* COLONEL CATH-CART *enters from another wearing his Indian headdress. The* CHAPLAIN *moves to him*]

CATHCART

It's a *great* idea! It might even get me into *Life* magazine. What are you staring at?

CHAPLAIN

Your hat. It's Indian.

132

CATHCART

Oh. These are all feathers in my cap. And soon I'm going to have one more. You've got a good man in Corporal Whitcomb. I hope you've got brains enough to appreciate *that*.

CHAPLAIN

Sergeant Whitcomb.

CATHCART

I *said* Sergeant Whitcomb. Did you steal a plum tomato from me? Corporal Whitcomb says you did.

CHAPLAIN

No, sir. You gave it to me.

CATHCART

Have you been writing Washington Irving's name on letters? Sergeant Whitcomb says you've been doing that, too.

CHAPLAIN

No, sir. I haven't.

CATHCART

I'm afraid I'm going to have to look into all of these charges more closely. In the meantime I want you and Corporal Whitcomb to write a sincere letter of condolence for me to the next of kin of every man who's killed, wounded, or missing in action. I want these letters filled with lots of personal details so there'll be no doubt I mean every word you say.

133

CHAPLAIN

Sir, that's impossible! We don't know all the men that well.

CATHCART

So what? Sergeant Whitcomb brought me this basic form letter that takes care of every situation. "Dear Mrs., Mr., Miss, or Mr. and Mrs. blank." Put in the name. "Words cannot express the deep personal grief I experienced when your husband, son, father, or brother was killed, wounded, or reported missing in action." I think that opening sentence sums up my sentiments exactly. Chaplain, maybe you'd better let Corporal Whitcomb run this whole program.

CHAPLAIN

Yes, sir. If you insist.

CATHCART

Good. Say! I think I'll volunteer the group for Avignon again.

CHAPLAIN

Avignon?

CATHCART

Why not? The sooner we get some casualties, the sooner we can make some progress on this.

[*Picks up phone*]

Get me Captain Black.

[*To* CHAPLAIN]

134

I'd like to get into the Christmas issue if we can.

[*Into telephone*]

Black? Colonel Cathcart. I've got good news for you!

[CAPTAIN BLACK *enters chortling as* CATHCART *and the* CHAPLAIN *leave*]

BLACK

Avignon? Eat your liver, boys. Ho, ho, ho. This time you bastards are really in for it.

[YOSSARIAN *and* MCWATT *enter, take parachute harnesses from the coat rack, and prepare for the mission*]

McWATT

Avignon? That's a scary one.

YOSSARIAN

That's where that radio gunner of mine was killed.

McWATT

I'm too nervous to pilot a plane anymore.

YOSSARIAN

Did you try Doc Daneeka?

McWATT

He made me take his pulse and feel his forehead. He always feels cold.

YOSSARIAN

I feel cold.

McWATT

He makes me put his name down on my log so he can collect flight pay without going into an airplane. He's afraid of crashing. He expects me to tell him why he's cold all the time.

YOSSARIAN

I'm not gonna go. Dammit, I've made up my mind.

McWATT

Okay. I won't go, either.

BLACK

Move along now, boys. It's time.

McWATT

Oh, well, what the hell. You ready?

YOSSARIAN

Yeah. Let's go. But one of these days . . .

[*They hurry off*]

BLACK

Eat your liver, you bastards. Eat your liver. Oh, how I hate you sons of bitches.

[*Exits as* GUS *and* WES *enter wearing white medical jackets and carrying some light medical paraphernalia*]

GUS

Poor McWatt.

WES

C'est la guerre. Oh, Christ. Look who's here.

[DOC DANEEKA *enters with a thermometer in his mouth*]

DOC DANEEKA

Ninety-six point eight. It isn't right to have this low temperature all the time. Can't you find anything wrong with me?

GUS

You're dead, sir.

WES

That's probably the reason you always feel so cold.

DOC DANEEKA

What are you talking about?

GUS

It's true, sir. The records show that you went up in McWatt's plane. There were no survivors, so you must have been killed.

WES

You ought to be glad you've got any temperature at all.

DOC DANEEKA

Have you both gone crazy? I'm going to report this to Sergeant Towser.

[DANEEKA *bolts out the doorway.* GUS *and* WES *leave in one direction as* SERGEANT TOWSER *enters from another*]

Sergeant Towser! Something terrible has happened.

TOWSER

I know. I'm sorry you're gone.

DOC DANEEKA

I'm not gone. I'm right here.

TOWSER

That's why I'm sorry. I don't know how I'm going to handle this one.

DOC DANEEKA

What do you suggest I do?

TOWSER

I suggest you keep out of sight until I find out how to dispose of your remains.

DOC DANEEKA

Remains?

TOWSER

Yes, sir. Perhaps after the War Department telegraphs your wife . . .

DOC DANEEKA

Oh, my God!

[DOC DANEEKA *hurries out.* TOWSER *follows.* WINTER-GREEN *enters reading a telegram*]

WINTERGREEN

[*Calling*]

Hey, lady! Here.

[DANEEKA's WIFE *enters.* WINTERGREEN *hands her the telegram.* DANEEKA *hurries in from the other side*]

DOC DANEEKA

I'm Doctor Daneeka.

WINTERGREEN

I've been reading all about you.

DOC DANEEKA

Has a telegram gone out yet? Has my wife been notified?

WINTERGREEN

[*Nodding*]

Doc, you can count on me. Your survivors are going to get everything that's coming to them.

DOC DANEEKA

What survivors? I'm right—

[MRS. DANEEKA *lets out a scream*]

139

MRS. DANEEKA

Mother! Ma! Oh!

[DANEEKA'S MOTHER-IN-LAW *enters and reads the telegram.* DANEEKA *sits at a desk and begins scribbling furiously*]

He's dead. He's dead.

MOTHER-IN-LAW

I never really liked him, anyway.

MRS. DANEEKA

What am I going to do?

[WINTERGREEN *hands a paper to* MOTHER-IN-LAW]

MOTHER-IN-LAW

Here's his G.I. Insurance policy for ten thousand dollars.

MRS. DANEEKA

It's not enough.

[DOC DANEEKA *finishes his letter and hands it to* WINTERGREEN.]

DOC DANEEKA

Please. Mail this out.

[WINTERGREEN *passes the letter to* MRS. DANEEKA]

MRS. DANEEKA

Mom! It's a mistake. He's alive. Isn't that wonderful?

MOTHER-IN-LAW

We'll have to give back the ten thousand.

MRS. DANEEKA

[*Writing*]

I don't care. "I was so happy to hear you're alive."

[*Seals letter and hands it to* WINTERGREEN]

He wants me to send a telegram to the War Department.

[*Hands telegram to* WINTERGREEN]

It was all an error. He's alive and well and happy.

[WINTERGREEN *bangs the letter with a rubber stamper and hands it back*]

MRS. DANEEKA

[*Reading*]

"Killed in action."

[WINTERGREEN *hands a telegram to* MOTHER-IN-LAW]

MOTHER-IN-LAW

"We regret to inform you there has been no error. Your husband is dead, dead as a doornail. Stop. You are undoubtedly the victim of some sadistic forger. We suggest you move. Stop. The president is sorry."

DOC DANEEKA
[*Returning*]

I'm expecting an important letter from my wife.

WINTERGREEN
[*Shakes his head*]

You're dead, Doc.

DOC DANEEKA
I've got to do something.

[*Exits*]

MRS. DANEEKA
What am I going to do?

MOTHER-IN-LAW
Keep the ten thousand.

WINTERGREEN
These might help.

[*Hands letters to them*]

MOTHER-IN-LAW
It's from the Veterans Administration. You're entitled to pension benefits for the rest of your natural life. Isn't that

wonderful? And to a burial allowance of two hundred and fifty dollars.

MRS. DANEEKA

Here's one from the Social Security Administration. It seems that under the provisions of the Old Age and Survivors Insurance Act of 1935 I'll receive monthly support for myself and the children until they reach the age of eighteen. And a burial allowance of two hundred and fifty dollars.

MOTHER-IN-LAW

[*From a drawer in the desk*]

Wow! Look at these. Three life insurance policies for fifty thousand each.

MRS. DANEEKA

Mother, I want you to know that all these hundreds of thousands of dollars are not worth a single penny to me without my devoted husband to share this good fortune with me.

WINTERGREEN

Aw, honey, that's no way to look at it. I'll bet your husband would want you to make a new life for yourself.

MRS. DANEEKA

I wouldn't know where to start.

WINTERGREEN

Get yourself some better clothes. That looks like a pretty nifty figure you've got there.

MOTHER-IN-LAW

And dye your hair blonde.

MRS. DANEEKA

Should I? I will.

WINTERGREEN

That's the spirit. Look at these.

MRS. DANEEKA

His fraternal lodge is giving us a cemetery plot. Isn't that sweet?

MOTHER-IN-LAW

His county medical association is giving him a burial allowance of two hundred and fifty dollars.

MRS. DANEEKA

Mother, I think it's just wonderful the way so many people are doing so much to help us bury him.

[DOC DANEEKA *enters*]

DOC DANEEKA

I'm having a terrible time trying to keep my head above the ground.

WINTERGREEN

Dust thou wert, and dust thou shall returnit.

[*The* CHAPLAIN *enters*]

144

CHAPLAIN

I'm doing everything I can to bring you back to life.

DOC DANEEKA

What's going to happen to me? They took away my tent. They took away my thermometer.

CHAPLAIN

Where do you live?

DOC DANEEKA

Outdoors. In the woods.

CHAPLAIN

Who does your laundry?

DOC DANEEKA

An Italian lady in a farmhouse.

CHAPLAIN

What do you do when it rains?

DOC DANEEKA

I get wet. Maybe I ought to give up. I'm losing my will to live.

CHAPLAIN

No, you mustn't give up. Write a letter to your wife. Plead with her to write directly to Colonel Cathcart. That way the truth will come out. And I'll go to Group Headquarters to see what I can do.

[CHAPLAIN *exits as* DOC DANEEKA *writes.* COLONEL KORN *strides in licking an envelope*]

KORN

I just told the Chaplain, and now I'll tell you. If I ever lay eyes on you again, I'll have you cremated on the spot.

[*To* WINTERGREEN]

Send this letter out immediately. It's from Colonel Cathcart.

[*Exits*]

DOC DANEEKA

Wintergreen, send this letter out immediately. It's my last chance.

WINTERGREEN

Sure, Doc.

[WINTERGREEN *takes the letter and hands it to* MRS. DANEEKA. *He hands* KORN's *letter to* DANEEKA'S MOTHER-IN-LAW]

MRS. DANEEKA

Mother, it's from him! He says he's alive. He wants me to write directly to his colonel for proof. Colonel Cathcart.

MOTHER-IN-LAW

Wait. This letter *is* from Colonel Cathcart.

MRS. DANEEKA

[*Taking the letter and reading aloud*]

"Dear Mrs., Mr., Miss, or Mr. and Mrs. Daneeka: Words cannot express the deep personal grief I experienced when your husband, son, father, or brother was killed, wounded, or reported missing in action."

MOTHER-IN-LAW

I think we ought to move.

[MRS. DANEEKA *nods, seals an envelope, and hands it back to* WINTERGREEN. *As they exit,* WINTERGREEN *passes the letter to* DOC DANEEKA]

DOC DANEEKA

Left no forwarding address, huh. Guess I might as well give up the ghost.

WINTERGREEN

That's the spirit.

[*As* DOC DANEEKA *exits, the* C.I.D. MAN *enters looking about with an air of suspicious authority and approaches* WINTERGREEN]

C.I.D. MAN

Hey, you! I'm looking for—

WINTERGREEN

I know, I know. I know everything. See Sergeant Towser in the orderly room.

[WINTERGREEN *leaves as* SERGEANT TOWSER *comes onstage. The* C.I.D. MAN *moves through the doorway and goes to him*]

C.I.D. MAN

I have to see Major Major right away. It's a matter of great secrecy and importance.

TOWSER

Will you have a seat?

C.I.D. MAN

Thank you, sergeant. Is he in?

TOWSER

Yes, sir. He is.

C.I.D. MAN

About how long will I have to wait?

TOWSER

Until he goes out.

C.I.D. MAN

Sergeant?

TOWSER

Sir?

C.I.D. MAN

What was that answer?

TOWSER

What was your question?

C.I.D. MAN

About how long will I have to wait before I can go in?

TOWSER

Just until he goes out to lunch. Then you can go right in.

C.I.D. MAN

But he won't be there then. Will he?

TOWSER

No, sir. But you can wait inside for him if you wish until he comes back.

C.I.D. MAN

When will he come back?

TOWSER

Right after lunch. Then you'll have to come out till he leaves for dinner. Major Major never sees anyone in his office while he's in his office.

C.I.D. MAN

Are you trying to make a fool out of me?

TOWSER

No, sir. Those are my orders. Major Major is always out when he's in. He's only in when he's out. You can ask him when you see him.

C.I.D. MAN

When can I see him?

TOWSER

Never.

C.I.D. MAN

[*Takes out a blackjack and seizes* SERGEANT TOWSER *by the shirtfront*]

You're under arrest.

TOWSER

What does that mean?

C.I.D. MAN

I'm a C.I.D. man, and you're my prisoner. Now you go inside and tell Major Major I want to see him and that I'm going to keep you under arrest until I do.

TOWSER

Yes, sir.

[SERGEANT TOWSER *moves timidly toward the other desk as* MAJOR MAJOR *climbs in through the window, removes his mustache and dark glasses, and sits down at the desk*]

Excuse me, sir. I'm under arrest.

MAJOR MAJOR

I thought I told you never to come in here.

TOWSER

Yes, sir. But there's a C.I.D. man outside who wants to see you. He's going to keep me under arrest until you see him. Won't you see him?

MAJOR MAJOR

Send him in.

TOWSER

Thank you, sir.

[*Returns to* C.I.D. MAN. MAJOR MAJOR *puts on his false mustache and sunglasses and hurries toward the window*]

It's all right, sir. Please go in.

[*The* C.I.D. MAN *bolts out the doorway suddenly and dashes around the furniture to the outside of the window. He gets there just as* MAJOR MAJOR *is ready to jump out*]

C.I.D. MAN

Major Major?

MAJOR MAJOR

No.

C.I.D. MAN

Then you're under arrest.

MAJOR MAJOR

Yes.

C.I.D. MAN

Then I have to talk to you.

MAJOR MAJOR

[*Removing his disguise*]

Okay. Go around again and come inside.

[C.I.D. MAN *starts away.* MAJOR MAJOR *climbs back inside his office. He puts on his mustache and glasses and dashes for the window again. The* C.I.D. MAN *dashes back around the furniture and reaches the window just in time to intercept him again.* MAJOR MAJOR *sighs in resignation*]

Okay. Come on in.

[*The* C.I.D. MAN *enters through the window.* MAJOR MAJOR *removes his mustache and sunglasses and sits down*]

C.I.D. MAN

I'm from the C.I.D. You're the only one in the squadron who knows.

MAJOR MAJOR

Sergeant Towser knows.

C.I.D. MAN

I had to tell him in order to see you. But he won't tell a soul.

MAJOR MAJOR

He told me.

C.I.D. MAN

'hat bastard. I'll throw a security check on him right away.
wouldn't leave any top-secret documents lying around if
were you.

MAJOR MAJOR

don't get any top-secret documents.

C.I.D. MAN

That's the kind I mean. Lock them in your cabinet where
Sergeant Towser can't get his hands on them.

MAJOR MAJOR

Sergeant Towser has the only key to the cabinet.

C.I.D. MAN

I'm afraid we're wasting time.

[*Removes some papers from his briefcase*]

Here's a copy of some censored mail that was tampered with
by the censoring officer. Can you make out his signature?

MAJOR MAJOR

Washington Irving.

C.I.D. MAN

Have you ever seen it before?

MAJOR MAJOR

No.

C.I.D. MAN

How about this one?

153

MAJOR MAJOR

Irving Washington.

[*He shakes his head*]

C.I.D. MAN

How about these? Official communications with your name on the routing list.

MAJOR MAJOR

I've never seen them before.

C.I.D. MAN

Is the man who signed these names in your squadron?

MAJOR MAJOR

I don't think there's a man with either of those two names in my squadron.

C.I.D. MAN

He's a lot cleverer than we thought. He's using a third name and posing as someone else. And I think I know what that name is.

[*Gives* MAJOR MAJOR *another paper*]

How about this?

MAJOR MAJOR

[*Reading*]

"Dear Mary. I yearn for you tragically. A. T. Tappman, Group Chaplain."

C.I.D. MAN

Do you know who A. T. Tappman is?

MAJOR MAJOR

He's the group chaplain.

C.I.D. MAN

That locks it up. Washington Irving is the group chaplain.

MAJOR MAJOR

A. T. Tappman is the group chaplain.

C.I.D. MAN

Are you sure?

MAJOR MAJOR

Yes.

C.I.D. MAN

Why should the group chaplain write this on a letter?

MAJOR MAJOR

Perhaps somebody else wrote it and forged his name.

C.I.D. MAN

Why should somebody want to forge the group chaplain's name?

MAJOR MAJOR

To escape detection.

C.I.D. MAN

You may be right. Maybe we're confronted with two men who have opposite names. One of them here in the squadron, one of them up at the hospital, and one of them with the chaplain. That makes three men, doesn't it? Are you absolutely sure you never saw any of these documents before?

MAJOR MAJOR

I would have signed them if I had.

C.I.D. MAN

With whose name? Yours or Washington Irving's?

) MAJOR MAJOR

With my own. I don't even know Washington Irving's name.

C.I.D. MAN

Major, I'm glad you're in the clear. We'll be able to work together. You keep your eyes open and let me know the minute you hear anyone even talking about Washington Irving. I'll throw a security check on the chaplain, Towser, and everyone else.

[*The* C.I.D. MAN *exits through the door. The* TEXAN, *wearing his maroon hospital bathrobe, appears on the stage and enters through the window*]

TEXAN

Who was that man?

MAJOR MAJOR

He's a C.I.D. Man.

TEXAN

Like hell he is! I'm the C.I.D. man around here.

[*Whining*]

I shouldn't even be here. I'm really a very sick man. I've got this terrible cough I can't shake.

MAJOR MAJOR

I'm very sorry.

TEXAN

A lot of good that does me. You haven't heard anyone talking about Washington Irving, have you?

MAJOR MAJOR

Yes. That man who was just in here. He was talking about Washington Irving.

TEXAN

Great! This might be just the break we need. You keep him under surveillance twenty-four hours a day while I rush back to the hospital and make my report.

[*The* TEXAN *climbs out through the window and runs off. A moment later the first* C.I.D. MAN *rushes in through the door*]

C.I.D. MAN

I just saw a man in a red bathrobe come jumping out your window and go running up the road! Didn't you see him?

MAJOR MAJOR

He was here talking to me.

C.I.D. MAN

I thought that looked mighty suspicious, a man jumping out the window in a red bathrobe. At first I thought it was you hightailing it for Mexico. But now I see it wasn't you. He didn't say anything about Washington Irving, did he?

MAJOR MAJOR

As a matter of fact he did.

C.I.D. MAN

Great! This might be just the break we need. Do you know where we can find him?

MAJOR MAJOR

At the hospital. He's really a very sick man.

C.I.D. MAN

That's marvelous. I'll go right up there after him. As a matter of fact I could use a checkup myself.

[*The* C.I.D. MAN *exits with a limp.* MAJOR MAJOR *watches him go, puts on his false mustache and enormous sunglasses, and climbs out the window. The* CHAPLAIN *enters, and the two come face to face*]

MAJOR MAJOR

I was coming to see you, Chaplain.

CHAPLAIN

I was coming to see you.

MAJOR MAJOR

I was coming to see you for help.

CHAPLAIN

I was coming to see *you* for help.

MAJOR MAJOR

Then there's not much point to it, is there?

[*Ducks his head down and scoots away offstage*]

CHAPLAIN

Dear wife. Is there a God, or is there not? Somehow, that great question is no longer as important to me as the simple question of good manners.

[YOSSARIAN *enters and joins him*]

YOSSARIAN

To die or not to die, *that* is *my* question. And I'm going crazy trying to answer it.

CHAPLAIN

Men have to die in a war. That's a matter of necessity.

YOSSARIAN

Yeah—but *which* men will die, though, is a matter of cir-cumstance. And I think I'm willing to be the victim of *anything* but circumstance. But . . . that's war, isn't it? Take Milo, for instance.

[MILO *enters carrying a small bouquet of flowers in one hand and a string of dried figs in the other*]

MILO

Me? I was in Smyrna getting figs.

YOSSARIAN

I thought you might have been at Avignon getting killed.

MILO

I wish I could have gone, but . . .

[*He shrugs*]

YOSSARIAN

Don't apologize, Milo. Didn't you fly fearlessly into the face of intense criticism by selling your cotton and ball bearings to the enemy?

MILO

At very good prices. Let me pass, please. I have business with Colonel Cathcart.

YOSSARIAN

I'll bet you do.

[*To the* CHAPLAIN *as he continues across stage with him and exits*]

'll bet Colonel Cathcart is *astonished* now every time Milo
comes to him and . . .

[MILO *moves through the doorway and approaches a desk,
while* COLONEL CATHCART *strides onstage rapidly in time
to receive him there.* MILO *hands him the bouquet of
flowers*]

CATHCART

For me?

MILO

Yes, sir. Sir, I'd like to fly more combat missions.

CATHCART

Milo, I am *astonished!* What in the world for?

MILO

I want to do my duty, sir.

CATHCART

But Milo, you are doing your duty. Who gave the men
chocolate-covered cotton?

MILO

Being a good mess officer in wartime just isn't enough.

CATHCART

Certainly it is, Milo. I don't know what's come over you.

MILO

[*Pointedly*]

Certainly it isn't. Some of the men are beginning to talk.

CATHCART

Oh, is that it? Give me their names, Milo. And I'll see to it
that they go on every dangerous mission.

MILO

No, Colonel. I'm afraid they're right.

CATHCART

How long have you been overseas now?

MILO

Eleven months, sir.

CATHCART

And how many missions have you flown?

MILO

Five.

CATHCART

Five?

MILO

Five, sir.

CATHCART

Five isn't very good, is it?

MILO

[*Sharply*]

Isn't it?

162

CATHCART

[*Correcting himself*]

On the contrary, five is very good, Milo. Five, you say? Just five?

MILO

Five.

CATHCART

And I'll bet that doesn't even include the time you bombed us.

MILO

Yes, sir. It does.

CATHCART

You didn't actually fly on that mission, if I remember correctly, did you?

MILO

But it was my mission, sir. I organized it.

CATHCART

Yes, Milo, of course. Five is *very* good. Why that averages out to . . . almost one combat mission every two months.

MILO

Many of the other men have seventy missions.

CATHCART

But they never produced any chocolate-covered cotton, did they? Milo, you're doing more than your share.

MILO

But they're getting all the medals. I want to win medals, too

CATHCART

People like you and me serve in different ways. Look at my own record. I'll bet it's not generally known, Milo, that I myself have flown only four missions, is it?

MILO

No, sir. It's generally known that you've flown only two missions.

CATHCART

All right, Milo. I can't praise you enough. I'll see that you're assigned to the next sixty-five missions so that you can have seventy, too.

MILO

Thank you, Colonel. You don't know what this means.

CATHCART

That's all right, Milo. I know just what this means.

MILO

[*Disagreeing pointedly*]

No, sir, you *don't* know what it means. I have figs in Smyrna.

CATHCART

So?

MILO

Someone will have to reap them. Someone else will have to

begin running the whole syndicate for me, take charge of the books, keep track of the records, look after the men, do buying and selling and shipping and storing and assume all responsibilities for—

CATHCART

Milo—

MILO

We've got cedars in Lebanon, zinc in Flint, and flint in Michigan—

CATHCART

Milo, wait—

MILO

—that must go from Atlanta to Holland to pay for the tulips to be shipped to Geneva to pay for the cheeses that must go to Vienna M.I.F.

CATHCART

M.I.F.?

MILO

Money in Front. And then there's the peas.

CATHCART

Peas?

MILO

That are on the high seas, the cork from New York, shoes for Toulouse, nails from Wales, and the ham for Siam.

CATHCART

Milo, stop!

MILO

We have coals in Newcastle, sir.

CATHCART

Milo, you can't fly sixty-five more missions! You can't even fly *one* more mission. You're like I am—*indispensable*!

MILO

[*Nodding contentedly*]

Sir, are you forbidding me to fly any more combat missions?

CATHCART

Milo, I forbid you to fly any more combat missions.

MILO

But that's not fair, sir. Why should I be penalized just because I'm a good mess officer?

CATHCART

I can't think of anything we can do about it.

MILO

Maybe we can get someone else to fly my missions for me.

CATHCART

But maybe we can get someone else to fly your missions for you!

MILO

Why not the men in the squadron, sir? After all, I'm doing all this for them.

CATHCART

Why not the men in the squadron? You're doing all this for them. They ought to be willing to do something for you in return.

MILO

What's fair is fair. They could take turns, sir.

CATHCART

They might even take turns.

MILO

Who gets the credit?

CATHCART

You get the credit, Milo. And if a man wins a medal flying one of your missions, you get the medal.

MILO

Who dies if he gets killed?

CATHCART

Why, he dies, of course. After all, Milo, what's fair is fair. There's just one thing.

MILO

You'll have to raise the number of missions.

CATHCART

I might have to raise the number of missions again. But this will be a good way to get that lousy rat Yossarian back into combat again.

MILO

Yossarian? Sir, Yossarian is a friend of mine. I'd give everything I own to Yossarian. But wait—since I don't own everything, I can't give everything I own to him, can I? So he'll just have to take his chances with the rest of the men, won't he?

CATHCART

We must never play favorites.

MILO

What's fair is fair.

CATHCART

And as long as I'm going to raise the missions again, I might as well raise them to good ones. I'm going to volunteer the men for Avignon again.

MILO

Avignon?

CATHCART

Sure, Milo. You don't want the men to fly easy, cowardly missions for you, do you?

MILO

I certainly do not. What kind of glory is that?

CATHCART

Good. I'm going to send them out to targets where you can be *proud* to wear those medals they earn for you.

[*Into telephone*]

Get me Captain Black. Black? This is Colonel Cathcart. Have I got good news for you!

[CAPTAIN BLACK *enters rubbing his hands with glee as* COLONEL CATHCART *walks off with* MILO]

BLACK

Avignon? Ho, ho, ho. Wait till those sons of bitches hear that. Oh, are they going to eat their livers now.

[YOSSARIAN *enters slowly and pauses at his parachute harness on the coat rack*]

YOSSARIAN

Eighty missions?

BLACK

That's right, you bastard. And do you know what this next one is? Avignon again. Okay, move along now.

[YOSSARIAN *hesitates and shakes his head*]

YOSSARIAN

No.

BLACK

No? What do you mean, no? Get going.

Yoss. refuses to go to Avignon

YOSSARIAN

Fuck you.

[YOSSARIAN *backs out glancing nervously over each shoulder.* BLACK *follows after him in amazement as a phone on the desk begins to ring.* COLONEL CATCHCART *hurries onstage in a violent emotional state wearing his Indian headdress and moves toward the desk to answer*]

CATHCART

[*Shouting*]

Korn! Korn!

[*He presses the loud bell for* KORN, *so there are two clangings before he picks up the phone*]

Yeah? I know, I know! Where is he now? Keep me informed.

[*Hangs up as* COLONEL KORN *enters leisurely, a feather in his shirt pocket*]

KORN

[*Dryly, as usual*]

You rang, sir?

CATHCART

Yes. We may be in terrible trouble. It's that bombardier Yossarian. He refuses to fly anymore.

KORN

Refuses? Who does he think he is? Achilles? Where is he now?

CATHCART

In the squadron, marching around backward. It's that damn Chaplain's fault. I told him to tell him to trust in God. Give me back the feather I gave you.

KORN

Marching backward? I suppose I'll have to think of something before the rest of the men start marching around backward, too.

CATHCART

Milo is talking to him. They're very good friends.

[YOSSARIAN *comes on stage walking backward and spinning continuously as he keeps whirling around to look over his shoulder.* MILO *enters with him and is forced to keep running in circles around him in order to converse with him*]

MILO

Yossarian, try to look at it this way. You'll be doing it for *me*, if not for yourself.

YOSSARIAN

Don't I know it!

MILO

Stand still, please. So we can discuss this like friends and gentlemen.

YOSSARIAN

Not a chance. I've got to cover my back.

MILO

I'll cover your back.

YOSSARIAN

Not a chance. I'm going.

[*Exits spinning*]

MILO

You'll be . . .

[*Spins dizzily through the doorway into the office, joining the* COLONELS]

. . . sorry! I can't tell you how disappointed I am in him.

KORN

Let's send him to Rome on a rest leave. He'll change his mind.

MILO

We can't even do that. He's already gone there.

KORN

Without a pass? That makes things so much easier for us. Can I have my feather back?

MILO

Are those feathers in your cap expensive?

CATHCART

These? Oh, they're very hard to come by. Where are you going?

MILO

Feathers.

[*Drifting away in a trance*]

Feathers. I'm going to corner the market on feathers.

CATHCART .

What an idea!

[*They exit after* MILO *as the* CHAPLAIN *enters alone. The* INVESTIGATING MAJOR *enters from a different direction and moves to the* CHAPLAIN]

CHAPLAIN

Dear wife. Someone must have been telling lies about me, for without having done anything wrong . . .

MAJOR

Chaplain Tappman?

CHAPLAIN

Yes?

[*The* TEXAN *enters from one direction, still in his hospital bathrobe; the* INVESTIGATING CAPTAIN *comes on from another carrying a folder; he is a cool, sinister man. The* CHAPLAIN *is surrounded*]

MAJOR

Come along.

CHAPLAIN

Where? Please—you're hurting my arm.

TEXAN

You'd better come along with us, Father.

CHAPLAIN

What have I done?

MAJOR

Why don't you keep your trap shut and let us ask the questions?

TEXAN

It isn't necessary to be so disrespectful.

MAJOR

Then tell him to keep his trap shut and let us ask the questions.

TEXAN

Father, please keep your trap shut and let us ask the questions.

MAJOR

It isn't necessary to call me Father. I'm not a Catholic.

TEXAN

Neither am I, Father. It's just that I'm a very devout person, and I like to call all men of God Father.

CHAPLAIN

Who are you?

[*They lead the* CHAPLAIN *through the doorway to one of the desks*]

TEXAN

We're from the government. That's a very serious crime you've committed, Father.

CHAPLAIN

What crime?

MAJOR

We don't know yet. But we sure know it's serious. Please make yourself comfortable.

[*The* MAJOR *takes a length of rubber hose from his brief-case and a box of matches. He strikes a match, holds the flame close to the* CHAPLAIN'*s face, and blows it out. He sets a metronome down and starts it ticking. He switches a lamp on and directs the beam into the* CHAPLAIN'*s face*]

We want you to relax.

TEXAN

You've got nothing to be afraid of, Father, if you're not guilty. What are you so afraid of? You're not guilty, are you?

CHAPLAIN

Guilty of what? What did I do?

MAJOR

Write your name for us, please. In your own handwriting.

[*To the* TEXAN]

See? They're not the same.

TEXAN

Father, I can't tell you how disappointed I am.

CHAPLAIN

For what?

MAJOR

This isn't your handwriting.

CHAPLAIN

But of course it is. Whose handwriting is it if not my own?

TEXAN

That's just what we aim to find out.

MAJOR

Talk, Chaplain.

CHAPLAIN

That handwriting is mine. Where else is my handwriting if not there?

CAPTAIN

Right here.

[*Tosses an envelope to the* CHAPLAIN]

Would you mind reading aloud what's written on that envelope?

CHAPLAIN

"Dear Mary. I yearn for you tragically. A. T. Tappman, Group Chaplain."

CAPTAIN

Do you know who wrote that?

CHAPLAIN

No.

MAJOR

Whoever did it signed his name.

CHAPLAIN

That's my name there.

MAJOR

Then you wrote it. Q.E.D.

CHAPLAIN

I didn't write it. That's not my handwriting, either.

MAJOR

Then you signed your name in somebody else's handwriting again.

CHAPLAIN

Oh, this is ridiculous! You've got no right to keep me here.

[*The* CHAPLAIN *jumps to his feet. The* MAJOR *pushes him down roughly*]

MAJOR

Okay, Captain. He's all yours.

CAPTAIN

[*Advancing toward the* CHAPLAIN]

Turn off the metronome, please. It's very annoying.

[*The* TEXAN *switches off the metronome*]

CHAPLAIN

Thank you. And the light, too, please.

CAPTAIN

Leave the light. That doesn't bother me. Chaplain, of what religious persuasion are you?

CHAPLAIN

I'm an Anabaptist, sir.

CAPTAIN

Doesn't the word *Anabaptist* simply mean that you're not a Baptist?

CHAPLAIN

Oh no, sir. There's much more.

CAPTAIN

Are you a Baptist?

CHAPLAIN

No, sir.

CAPTAIN

Then you are *not* a Baptist, are you? You could easily be . . . Washington Irving, couldn't you?

CHAPLAIN

Washington Irving?

MAJOR

Come on, Washington. Why don't you make a clean breast of it? We know you stole that plum tomato.

CHAPLAIN

Oh, now I'm beginning to understand. I didn't steal that plum tomato, sir. Colonel Cathcart gave it to me.

MAJOR

Are you calling a superior officer a liar?

TEXAN

Is that why you tried to give it to Sergeant Whitcomb, Father? Because it was a hot tomato?

CHAPLAIN

No, no, no. Because I didn't want it.

CAPTAIN

Why'd you steal it if you didn't want it?

CHAPLAIN

I didn't steal it!

CAPTAIN

Why are you so guilty, if you didn't steal it?

CHAPLAIN

I'm not guilty!

CAPTAIN

Why would we be questioning you if you weren't guilty?

CHAPLAIN

Oh, I don't know.

MAJOR

He thinks we have time to waste.

CAPTAIN

Chaplain, I have here in my hand a signed statement from Sergeant Whitcomb in which he states he knew the tomato was hot from the way you tried to unload it on him.

CHAPLAIN

I swear to God I didn't steal it, sir. I give you my word it was not a hot tomato.

MAJOR

Why don't we knock his goddamn brains out?

TEXAN

Yeah, we could do that. He's only an Anabaptist.

CAPTAIN

No, we've got to find him guilty first. Chaplain, we charge you with being Washington Irving and taking unlicensed liberties in censoring the letters of officers and enlisted men. Are you guilty or innocent?

CHAPLAIN

Innocent, sir.

MAJOR

Guilty.

TEXAN

Guilty.

CAPTAIN

That's two to one, so guilty it is, then. Chaplain, we accuse you, also, of the commission of crimes and infractions we don't even know about yet. Guilty or innocent?

CHAPLAIN

How can I say if you don't tell me what they are?

CAPTAIN

How can we tell you if we don't know?

MAJOR

Guilty.

TEXAN

Sure he's guilty. If they're his crimes and infractions, he must have committed them.

CAPTAIN

Guilty it is, then. He's all yours, Major.

MAJOR

Okay, Chaplain. You heard the verdict. Get the hell out of here.

CHAPLAIN

Aren't you even going to punish me?

MAJOR

Damn right. But we're certainly not going to let you hang around while we decide how to do it. So beat it. Go on, hit the road.

CHAPLAIN

I'm free to go?

MAJOR

You can go. But you're certainly not free. Is he?

[*The three exit chuckling*]

CHAPLAIN

Dear wife. Perhaps I have begun to imagine things. If so, I am imagining things that I have imagined before, because I seem to be imagining everything twice. Yossarian has gone away to Rome . . .

[YOSSARIAN *enters and walks along with the* CHAPLAIN]

YOSSARIAN

Rome was in ruins when I got there. There was rubble at the airport. The Colosseum was a dilapidated shell, and the Arch of Constantine had fallen. I missed Nurse Duckett in Rome. I missed Luciana. I went looking for Nately's whore . . .

[YOSSARIAN *moves toward the doorway as the* CHAPLAIN *continues across the stage and exits. The* OLD WOMAN *enters, sits in a chair, and begins to rock and moan*]

OLD WOMAN

Gone.

YOSSARIAN

Where?

OLD WOMAN

Away. Chased away into the street. All the poor young girls.

YOSSARIAN

By who? Who did it?

OLD WOMAN

The tall soldiers with the hard white hats and clubs.

YOSSARIAN

Did they arrest them?

OLD WOMAN

They chased them away. Who will take care of me?

YOSSARIAN

What right did they have?

OLD WOMAN

Catch–22.

YOSSARIAN

What?

OLD WOMAN

Catch–22. Catch–22 says they have a right to do anything we can't stop them from doing.

YOSSARIAN

How did you know it was Catch–22? Did they show it to you? Did they let you read it?

OLD WOMAN

They don't have to show us Catch–22. The law says they don't have to.

YOSSARIAN

What law says they don't have to?

OLD WOMAN

Catch–22.

YOSSARIAN

Oh, damn! I bet it isn't even there. Where's the old man? The one that said he was going to live forever?

OLD WOMAN

Dead. One minute he was living, one minute he was dead.

YOSSARIAN

Nately's girl friend?

OLD WOMAN

Gone. Chased away with all the rest. They would not even let them take their coats.

YOSSARIAN

Who will take care of her?

OLD WOMAN

Who will take care of me?

[YOSSARIAN *puts money in her lap*]

It's not enough.

YOSSARIAN

It's all I have.

OLD WOMAN

Money is not enough.

YOSSARIAN

Money is all I have.

OLD WOMAN

Catch–22.

YOSSARIAN

Mother, there's no such thing.

OLD WOMAN

Come?

YOSSARIAN

It doesn't exist. But that makes no difference, because every-one thinks it does.

OLD WOMAN

Who will take care of me?

YOSSARIAN

No one.

VOICE

[*Offstage*]

Arf, arf! Arf, arf, arf!

YOSSARIAN

There was no one I knew in Rome but Aarfy, our lead navigator, who had never been able to find himself since leaving college. And the unattractive little maid who took care of our apartment, whom none of the men had ever wanted, none of the men but Aarfy, who . . .

[YOSSARIAN *stops and stares ahead offstage with a look of incredulous horror*]

Oh, my God! I won't believe it.

VOICE

[*Offstage*]

Arf, arf!

[AARFY *saunters onstage amid the beds and chairs and gazes placidly through the window at* YOSSARIAN]

YOSSARIAN

Aarfy!

[*Rushes upstage directly to* AARFY *and pulls him around roughly*]

What the *hell* did you do?

AARFY

[*Barking jokingly*]

Arf, Arf! Arf!

YOSSARIAN

Stop it—for Christ sake!

AARFY

Arf! Relax, Yossarian. It's just the maid. I only raped her once.

YOSSARIAN

You killed her, too! You threw her out the window!

AARFY

Oh, I had to kill her after I raped her. I couldn't let her go around saying bad things about us, could I?

YOSSARIAN

Why did you have to touch her at all? Why didn't you go to a prostitute, if it came to that?

Catch Yoss.

AARFY

Oh, no, not me. I never paid for it in my life.

YOSSARIAN

Aarfy, are you insane? You *murdered* a girl. They're going to put you in jail.

AARFY

Oh no, not me. Not good old Aarfy. I hardly think they're going to make too much of a fuss over one Italian servant girl. Do you?

YOSSARIAN

Listen.

[*Sirens sound and approach*]

Aarfy, they're coming to arrest you. Don't you understand? You can't take the life of another human being.

AARFY

[*Lamely*]

Oh, no, not me. They're not coming to arrest good old Aarfy. Not good old Aarfy.

[*Two* MP's *enter.* AARFY *whimpers and shrinks back in fear as they stride through the door. They pass* AARFY *and seize* YOSSARIAN]

MP

Captain Yossarian? You're under arrest.

188

YOSSARIAN

Me? For what?

MP

You're absent without official leave. You left your base without a pass.

YOSSARIAN

But he—

MP

Never mind him. Let's go.

[*To* AARFY, *saluting*]

Sorry, sir. Forgive the intrusion.

AARFY

That's quite all right. Hey, Yo-Yo.

[*Gloating, and with an obscene Italian gesture*]

Arf, arf!

[AARFY *breaks into wild, barking laughter and leaves as the* MP's *march* YOSSARIAN *out the doorway and around the circle of furniture.* COLONEL CATHCART *walks in carrying a bunch of feathers and a stack of black eyes. The bell rings clangorously*]

CATHCART

Korn! Korn!

KORN

[*Dryly, as he enters*]

You rang, sir?

CATHCART

Dammit, Korn! I'm getting sick and tired of that joke.

KORN

Forgive me, sir. You should of mentioned it.

CATHCART

I've got a pile of black eyes and a big bunch of feathers for my cap, and I don't know which I'm going to need more of. Will you handle him?

KORN

Of course. Would you like a fig?

[COLONEL CATHCART *shakes his head. The* MP's *march* YOSSARIAN *around through the doorway and lead him inside just as* KORN, *munching on a fig, sits down comfortably on a desk to await him*]

MP

Sir, we are pleased to report that the prisoner Yossarian—

KORN

Get out.

MP

Thank you, sir.

[MP's *exit*]

KORN

Yossarian, huh? Do you know what we're going to do to you? We're going to send you home.

YOSSARIAN

You're kidding.

KORN

No. But . . . there's a catch.

YOSSARIAN

Twenty-two?

KORN

Of course. Would you like a fig? We can't simply send you home for refusing to fly more missions and expect the rest of the men to continue, can we? So we've worked out this little deal.

YOSSARIAN

What kind of deal?

KORN

Odious. But you'll accept it quickly enough.

YOSSARIAN

Don't be too sure.

KORN

It's that or a court-martial. You'd leave us no alternative . . .

[*Emphasizing the words delightedly for the distress he knows they will cause* COLONEL CATHCART]

. . . even though it might turn out to be a terrible black eye for Colonel Cathcart.

CATHCART

Goddamn it—I hate this cigarette holder! I wonder if it's doing me any good.

KORN

It's a feather in your cap with General Peckem, but a black eye for you with General Dreedle.

CATHCART

Which one am I supposed to please?

KORN

Both.

CATHCART

How?

KORN

By sending this man home a hero and getting all the others to fly more missions.

CATHCART

I want to be a general!

KORN

[*To* YOSSARIAN]

And there you have it. Everyone teaches us to aspire to higher things. A general is higher than a colonel, so we're oth aspiring. Won't you help us by doing everything you're ordered to? This is your last chance to say yes.

YOSSARIAN

No.

KORN

In that case we're going to have to send you home. Just do a few things for us, and—

YOSSARIAN

What things?

KORN

Oh, tiny insignificant things. We will issue orders returning you to the States—really, we will, safe and sound—and all you have to do in return is . . .

YOSSARIAN

What?

KORN

Like us.

YOSSARIAN

Like you?

KORN

That's right. Like us. Join us. Be our pal. Say nice things about us.

YOSSARIAN

That's all?

KORN

That's all.

YOSSARIAN

That isn't going to be too easy.

KORN

Oh, it will be a lot easier than you think. We're going to promote you to major and give you a medal. You'll have big parades in your honor and make lots of speeches.

YOSSARIAN

I'm not sure I want to make speeches.

KORN

Then we'll forget the speeches. We just don't want anyone to know there's ever been any friction between us.

YOSSARIAN

Suppose I denounce you when I get back to the States?

KORN

Why should you want to? You're going to be one of the boys now, remember? You'd have to be a fool to throw it all away for just a moral principle.

YOSSARIAN

That's a pretty scummy trick I'd be playing on the rest of the men, isn't it?

KORN

Odious.

194

YOSSARIAN

ut what the hell! Let them stand up and do something bout it the way I did. Right?

KORN

)f course.

YOSSARIAN

There's no reason I have to risk my life for them, is there?

KORN

Of course not.

YOSSARIAN

It's a deal!

KORN

Welcome aboard.

[*They all shake hands.* NATELY'S WHORE *tiptoes on stage in an army jacket carrying a long knife. She stations herself outside the doorway, hiding the knife*]

YOSSARIAN

Thanks, Colonel. I—

KORN

Call me Blackie, John. We're pals now, remember? Have a fig.

YOSSARIAN

Sure, Blackie. My friends call me Yo-Yo. Blackie, I—

KORN

His friends call him Yo-Yo. Why don't you congratulat
Yo-Yo on what a sensible move he's making?

CATHCART

That's a real sensible move you're making, Yo-Yo.

YOSSARIAN

Thank you, Colonel, I—

KORN

Call him Chuck.

CATHCART

Sure, call me Chuck. We're all pals now.

YOSSARIAN

Sure, Chuck.

CATHCART

Come on over for dinner with us some night, Yo-Yo. In the
group dining room. How about tonight?

YOSSARIAN

I'd love to, sir.

KORN

[*Correcting him genially*]

Chuck.

Stabbed by whore

YOSSARIAN

'm sorry, Blackie. Chuck. I can't get used to it.

CATHCART

That's all right, pal.

KORN

Sure, pal.

YOSSARIAN

Thanks, pal.

CATHCART

Don't mention it, pal.

KORN

So long, pal. Exit smiling.

[YOSSARIAN *exits through the doorway laughing.* NATELY'S WHORE *salutes him*]

YOSSARIAN

Hi. Say, don't I know you from—

[*She stabs him under the arm.* YOSSARIAN *sinks down in pain*]

I've been looking all over for—

[*Screaming, as she raises the knife to stab him again*]

—oh, nooo!

[*The* COLONELS *rush out.* NATELY'S WHORE *runs off They chase after her.*]

[YOSSARIAN *staggers to a bed clutching his wound and collapses.*]

[TWO DOCTORS *and* NURSE DUCKETT *enter to treat him. They carry medical equipment*]

FIRST DOCTOR

Okay. Cut.

SECOND DOCTOR

You cut.

YOSSARIAN

[*Sitting up*]

No cuts.

FIRST DOCTOR

Now look who's butting in. Are we going to operate or aren't we?

NURSE DUCKETT

He doesn't need an operation. Just stop the bleeding and put a few stitches in.

FIRST DOCTOR

But I've never had a chance to operate before. Which one is the scalpel? Is this one the scalpel?

Doctor's

SECOND DOCTOR

The other one. Well, go ahead and cut if you want to. Make the incision.

YOSSARIAN

[*Sitting up again*]

No incisions.

FIRST DOCTOR

Is he going to keep talking that way while I operate on him?

NURSE DUCKETT

You can't operate until I admit him.

[INVESTIGATING MAJOR *enters*]

MAJOR

You can't admit him until I clear him.

[INVESTIGATING CAPTAIN *enters*]

CAPTAIN

You can't clear him until I investigate him.

[*To* YOSSARIAN]

Where were you born?

YOSSARIAN

On a battlefield.

MAJOR

No, no. In what state?

YOSSARIAN

In a state of innocence.

MAJOR

You don't understand.

CAPTAIN

Let me handle him.

[*To* YOSSARIAN]

Are you a smart aleck or something?

NURSE DUCKETT

He's still bleeding. He might even die.

MAJOR

Good for him.

CAPTAIN

It would serve the finky bastard right. All right, John, let's speak out. We want to get to the truth.

YOSSARIAN

Everyone calls me Yo-Yo.

MAJOR

We want you to cooperate with us, Yo-Yo. We're your friends, and we want you to trust us. We're here to help you.

CAPTAIN

Let's jab our thumb down inside his wound and gouge it.

[YOSSARIAN *groans and lets his eyes fall closed*]

FIRST DOCTOR

He's fainted. Can't we treat him now?

MAJOR

I hope the bastard does die.

CAPTAIN

I hate the sight of blood.

[*They exit*]

NURSE DUCKETT

[*Whispering*]

Aren't you ashamed of yourself?

YOSSARIAN

No. Don't go.

NURSE DUCKETT

I'm through with you. I want to marry a doctor.

FIRST DOCTOR

Then let's start. I'm raring to operate. Should I wash my hands first?

YOSSARIAN

No operations.

SECOND DOCTOR

Can't you make him shut up? You're his girl.

NURSE DUCKETT

Not anymore. I could give him a total and knock him out.

SECOND DOCTOR

At least we'd have some quiet.

FIRST DOCTOR

Then I can take out his liver.

YOSSARIAN

No totals.

SECOND DOCTOR

There he goes again.

FIRST DOCTOR

Can I take out his liver?

NURSE DUCKETT

You can stitch up his wound.

FIRST DOCTOR

I'd rather take out his liver. Come on—knock him out.

YOSSARIAN

Don't knock me—

[NURSE DUCKETT *covers his face with an ether cone.*
YOSSARIAN *sinks back unconscious.* NURSE DUCKETT *and
the* DOCTORS *bend over him a moment and start away*]

NURSE DUCKETT

We were never more than just friends.

[*They exit in one direction as* COLONEL KORN *comes in
from another, munching on a fig*]

YOSSARIAN

[*Aloud, to himself*]

She wants to marry a doctor.

KORN

The deal is still on. We've got this wonderful cover story
about a Nazi assassin who—

[YOSSARIAN *grabs for* KORN, *misses, and begins retching
loudly*]

KORN

[*With a grimace of disgust*]

How vulgar!

[*Exits as* NURSE DUCKETT *returns*]

YOSSARIAN

What's happening to me?

NURSE DUCKETT

I'm going to marry a doctor.

YOSSARIAN

Which doctor?

NURSE DUCKETT

Any doctor. My mother wouldn't like you. Neither would her friends.

YOSSARIAN

Is that so important?

NURSE DUCKETT

We can still be friends.

YOSSARIAN

Friends?

NURSE DUCKETT

Nurse and patient, I mean. Give me a ring sometime when you need anything. Tee-hee-hee.

[*Exits laughing at her own joke as the* INVESTIGATING CAPTAIN *enters wearing a bathrobe over his uniform*]

CAPTAIN

We've got your pal, buddy. We've got your pal.

YOSSARIAN

What are you talking about?

CAPTAIN

[*Leaving*]

You know.

YOSSARIAN

Who's my pal?

CHAPLAIN

[*Entering*]

Maybe I'm your pal. Yossarian, we're all very proud of you.

YOSSARIAN

Proud?

CHAPLAIN

For risking your life to save Colonel Cathcart from that Nazi assassin.

YOSSARIAN

That was no Nazi assassin. That was Nately's whore. And she was trying to kill me.

CHAPLAIN

The official report says—

YOSSARIAN

It's part of the deal.

CHAPLAIN

What deal?

YOSSARIAN

The deal I made with Colonel Cathcart and Colonel Korn. They'll let me go home a big hero if I say nice things about them and never criticize them for making the rest of the men fly more missions.

CHAPLAIN

But that's shameful! Isn't it?

YOSSARIAN

Odious is the word we agreed on. It's that or a court-martial. They'd lock me in prison with a bunch of criminals.

CHAPLAIN

You can't let them do that.

YOSSARIAN

Then maybe I'll fly more missions.

CHAPLAIN

You might get killed.

YOSSARIAN

Then I guess I won't. A funny thing happened before— maybe I dreamed it. I think a strange man came in here and told me he's got my pal. "We've got your pal," he said. He scared me.

[*Near tears*]

They've got all my pals, haven't they?

texan-bathrobe

CHAPLAIN

There, there. Try to sleep now. I'll be back.

[*Tiptoes out one side as* WHITCOMB *enters from another carrying a letter. He takes* YOSSARIAN's *pulse*]

WHITCOMB

[*Tearing up the letter*]

Shit!

[*To the* TEXAN, *who enters in his hospital robe as* WHITCOMB *leaves*]

He's going to live.

TEXAN

[*Seating himself beside the bed*]

Hi. Hey, wake up.

YOSSARIAN

You're still in here, aren't you?

TEXAN

I'm glad you're alive.

YOSSARIAN

Why?

TEXAN

So I can slit your throat for you from ear to ear.

207

threaten to
kill Yoss s -pal
(texan + capt.)

YOSSARIAN

[*Terrified*]

What are you talking about?

TEXAN

One time when you're sound asleep, I'm going to tiptoe in here very quietly and slit your throat for you from ear to ear.

YOSSARIAN

Why?

TEXAN

Why not?

YOSSARIAN

Why are you sitting here?

TEXAN

I'm waiting for you to fall asleep, so I can slit your throat for you from ear to ear.

YOSSARIAN

Help!

[NURSE DUCKETT *hurries in*]

TEXAN

[*Leaving*]

He's delirious, I think.

208

YOSSARIAN

He's going to slit my throat for me from ear to ear.

NURSE DUCKETT

No, he's not. They're going to disappear you.

YOSSARIAN

What does that mean?

NURSE DUCKETT

I don't know. I heard them talking.

YOSSARIAN

Who?

NURSE DUCKETT

I don't know. I just heard them say they were going to disappear you.

YOSSARIAN

It doesn't make sense. It isn't even good grammar. What the hell does it mean when they disappear somebody?

NURSE DUCKETT

[*Plaintively*]

I don't know.

YOSSARIAN

You're a great help!

209

NURSE DUCKETT

Why are you picking on me? I only came here to warn you.

YOSSARIAN

I'm sorry.

[*Tries to embrace her*]

NURSE DUCKETT

[*Pulling away*]

Don't.

YOSSARIAN

What should I do?

[NURSE DUCKETT *shrugs and leaves by one side as the* INVESTIGATING CAPTAIN *returns from another*]

YOSSARIAN

Did you come to disappear me?

CAPTAIN

We've got your pal, buddy. We've got your pal.

YOSSARIAN

What the *hell* are you talking about?

CAPTAIN

You'll find out, buddy. You'll find out.

[YOSSARIAN *lunges at him and misses. The* CAPTAIN *laughs and steps away*]

YOSSARIAN

You give me chills.

CAPTAIN

[*Moving away*]

Good.

YOSSARIAN

[*Rising to follow him*]

You make my blood run cold.

CAPTAIN

I'm glad.

[*Exits as* SNOWDEN *appears on stage in combat clothes. Doubled over, clutching his abdomen in pain, he sinks to the floor*]

SNOWDEN

[*Moaning*]

I'm cold.

YOSSARIAN

[*Turning back*]

I'm freezing.

SNOWDEN

I'm cold. I'm cold.

Adam Arkin as Snowden. John Pleshette as Yossarian.
"I'm cold."
"There, there."

[YOSSARIAN *notices him with surprise. He hangs his bathrobe on the coat rack and puts on a parachute harness. He takes a first-aid kit from the coat rack and moves across the stage to* SNOWDEN]

SNOWDEN

'm cold.

YOSSARIAN

You're going to be all right, kid. You're going to be all right.

SNOWDEN

I'm cold. I'm cold.

YOSSARIAN

There, there. There, there.

SNOWDEN

I'm cold. I'm cold.

YOSSARIAN

There, there. There, there.

[YOSSARIAN *kneels, opens the first-aid kit, and begins treating* SNOWDEN *for his thigh wound.* SNOWDEN *moans*]

Did I hurt you?

SNOWDEN

I'm cold. I'm cold.

YOSSARIAN

There, there. There, there.

Snowden is
cold. Yoss cares for
him

SNOWDEN

I'm scared.

YOSSARIAN

You're not in any danger. The bleeding stopped. All I've got to do is bandage you up and keep you warm until the plane lands.

SNOWDEN

It's starting to hurt me!

YOSSARIAN

I'll give you a shot of morphine. I'll give you a double shot.

[*Removes a box from the first-aid kit, opens it, and finds only a slip of paper inside*]

Milo Minderbinder, you bastard!

[*To* SNOWDEN]

There is no morphine.

[*Reading*]

"What's good for Milo Minderbinder is good for the country."

SNOWDEN

[*Moaning*]

I'm cold.

YOSSARIAN

I've got two aspirins.

SNOWDEN

[*Shaking his head*]

I'm cold. I'm cold.

YOSSARIAN

It's very warm. It's very warm here in the plane.

SNOWDEN

I'm cold.

YOSSARIAN

I'm scared!

SNOWDEN

I'm cold.

YOSSARIAN

The edges of your mouth, they're turning blue. How do you feel?

SNOWDEN

Cold. I'm cold.

YOSSARIAN

You're going to be all right. There's no more bleeding.

SNOWDEN

I'm cold. I'm cold.

YOSSARIAN

There, there. There, there. We'll be back on the groun soon. You're going to be okay.

[SNOWDEN *shakes his head and points with his chin dow toward his armpit.* YOSSARIAN *opens* SNOWDEN's *flak suit gapes in horror, and screams wildly*]

SNOWDEN

I'm cold.

[YOSSARIAN *forces himself to look again. He screams a second time and squeezes both hands over his eyes*]

I'm cold. I'm cold.

YOSSARIAN

I'm cold. I'm cold, too.

SNOWDEN

I'm cold. I'm cold.

YOSSARIAN

[*Holding* SNOWDEN]

There, there. There, there.

SNOWDEN

I'm cold. I'm cold.

YOSSARIAN

There, there. There, there.

SNOWDEN

m cold.

[*He dies*]

YOSSARIAN

`here, there. You're going to be all . . .

[*He realizes Snowden is dead and lowers him to the floor*]

There, there.

[*The* CHAPLAIN *enters.* YOSSARIAN, *rising slowly, addresses the* CHAPLAIN *as he moves away from* SNOWDEN]

There was God's plenty, all right—liver, lungs, kidneys, ribs, stomach, and bits of the stewed tomatoes Snowden had eaten that day for lunch.

[*He goes to the coat rack and takes off his parachute harness*]

I hate stewed tomatoes. All this time I had been treating Snowden for the wrong wound. I wondered how in the world to begin to save him now. There was Snowden's secret, and he had spilled it all over the messy floor of the airplane. It was easy to read the message in his entrails. Man was matter, that was Snowden's secret. Drop him out a window and he'll fall. Set fire to him and he'll burn. Bury him and he'll rot, like other kinds of garbage. The spirit gone, man is garbage.

CHAPLAIN

I know.

YOSSARIAN

That was Snowden's secret. Ripeness is all.

[*Returns to the bed*]

CHAPLAIN

Major is here.

YOSSARIAN

Major who?

CHAPLAIN

Major. Major Major. He has to speak to you.

[MAJOR MAJOR *enters without disguise and moves hesitantly toward the doorway*]

YOSSARIAN

Chaplain, help me! Get the rest of my clothes.

CHAPLAIN

Where? How will I get them?

YOSSARIAN

I don't know. Ask Nurse Duckett. She'll do anything she can to be rid of me.

CHAPLAIN

What are you going to do?

talks Maj Maj to Yoss

YOSSARIAN

I don't know. But hurry. Please. For once in your life *succeed* at something.

[*The* CHAPLAIN *leaves.* MAJOR MAJOR *enters through the doorway and approaches* YOSSARIAN]

Who the hell are you?

[*With a lame smile,* MAJOR MAJOR *puts his mustache and glasses on, then removes them*]

Where'd *you* come from?

MAJOR MAJOR

Colonel Korn made me come here to talk to you. He says you disgust him. He says I disgust him, too. He wants me to tell you that the deal is still on.

YOSSARIAN

No, it isn't. I'm breaking it.

MAJOR MAJOR

Oh, dear. Why did you agree to it if you didn't like it?

YOSSARIAN

I did it in a moment of weakness. I wanted to save my life.

MAJOR MAJOR

They're going to court-martial you.

YOSSARIAN

[*Laughs and thumbs his nose*]

No, they won't. Please don't lie to me. There's an officia
report that says I was stabbed by a Nazi assassin.

MAJOR MAJOR

But, Yossarian! There's another official report that says you
were stabbed in the course of black-market operations involving the sale of military secrets to the enemy.

YOSSARIAN

Another official report?

MAJOR MAJOR

Yossarian, they can prepare as many official reports as they
need. Didn't you know that?

YOSSARIAN

Oh, dear. What a clear way you have of describing things.

MAJOR MAJOR

Please don't blame me. I'm only trying to help you.

YOSSARIAN

That's what that nice detective said before he decided to
jab his thumb into my wound.

MAJOR MAJOR

I'm not a detective. I'm a college professor who's trying to
serve his country. And I wouldn't lie to anyone.

YOSSARIAN

What would you do if one of the men in the squadron asked you about this conversation?

MAJOR MAJOR

I would lie to him.

YOSSARIAN

Look what they've done to us. How can you work for them?

MAJOR MAJOR

I try not to think of them. I try to think only of my country.

YOSSARIAN

Christ, Major, don't tell *me* that. I've flown seventy Goddamn missions. But that war's over. The country's not in danger anymore. But *I* am. From Cathcart and Korn.

MAJOR MAJOR

Then let them send you home. It's a way to save yourself.

YOSSARIAN

It's a way to lose myself. Goddammit! I can't join those bastards now. Getting stabbed by that bitch was the best thing that ever happened to me.

MAJOR MAJOR

Would you rather go to jail? Or fly more missions?

YOSSARIAN

What would you do?

MAJOR MAJOR

Me?

YOSSARIAN

Would you let them send you home?

MAJOR MAJOR

No. I don't think so. Not under those conditions. But I certainly wouldn't let them send me to jail.

YOSSARIAN

Then you'd fly more missions?

MAJOR MAJOR

No, of course not. That would be total capitulation. And I might get killed.

YOSSARIAN

Then you'd run away? Desert?

MAJOR MAJOR

Oh, no. I don't think I could do that. There'd be no hope for me, would there?

YOSSARIAN

No. No hope for us at all?

MAJOR MAJOR

No hope at all. There just doesn't seem to be anything you can do, is there?

YOSSARIAN

No.

[*Perking up with an idea*]

222

And that's good. Since there's nothing I can do, I know just what I *can* do.

MAJOR MAJOR

What?

YOSSARIAN

I'm going to run away.

MAJOR MAJOR

Where?

YOSSARIAN

To Sweden!

MAJOR MAJOR

Sweden? You'll never get there.

YOSSARIAN

No. But I can get to Rome easily enough—if you keep your mouth shut long enough for me to catch a ride. And I can take my chances from there.

MAJOR MAJOR

No, no, no. Yossarian, you can't run away. You'll always be alone. You'll always live in danger.

YOSSARIAN

I live *that* way now.

[*The* CHAPLAIN *enters carrying a pillowcase stuffed with clothing and a musette bag*]

223

CHAPLAIN

Yossarian! Guess what! I got them, I got them.

YOSSARIAN

You see, Major? There is hope.

MAJOR MAJOR

Chaplain, please talk to him, will you? He's deserting. He wants to run away to Sweden.

CHAPLAIN

Wonderful! Run away to Sweden, Yossarian. And I'll stay here and persevere. Yes, I'll stay here and—

MAJOR MAJOR

Chaplain, will you please shut up? Yossarian, listen. You'll never make it. It's almost a geographical impossibility to get to Sweden from here.

YOSSARIAN

Hell, Major, I know that. But at least I'll be trying.

MAJOR MAJOR

It's absolutely insane. Your conscience will never let you rest.

YOSSARIAN

God bless it. I wouldn't want to live in this world without strong misgivings.

MAJOR MAJOR

Chaplain, can't *you* do something?

CHAPLAIN

Yes. I'm going to punch Captain Black in the nose.

[*He shadowboxes*]

Pow! Just like that.

[NATELY'S WHORE *appears on stage, eavesdrops, and stealthily positions herself just outside the door carrying a long knife*]

YOSSARIAN

Well, Major? Do you think you can disappear again long enough for me to catch a ride?

MAJOR MAJOR

It's my duty to stop you.

YOSSARIAN

Are you going to try?

MAJOR MAJOR

What would you do? Beat me up?

YOSSARIAN

Why do you say that?

[*The* CHAPLAIN, *feinting punches, shadowboxes close to* MAJOR MAJOR]

CHAPLAIN

I will beat you up. You and Corporal Whitcomb and maybe

even Colonel Cathcart. Wouldn't it be wonderful if I found
I didn't have to be afraid anymore?

YOSSARIAN

Are you going to stop me?

MAJOR MAJOR

[*Reaching his decision*]

No, of course not! Go, for God sakes, and hurry! Do you
need money?

YOSSARIAN

I've got money.

MAJOR MAJOR

Here's more.

CHAPLAIN

Good-by, Yossarian. And good luck. I'll stay here and
persevere.

YOSSARIAN

[*Starting away toward the door*]

So long, Chaplain. Thanks, Major.

MAJOR MAJOR

How do you feel?

YOSSARIAN

Fine. No, I'm frightened.

226

MAJOR MAJOR

That's good. It proves you're still alive. It won't be fun.

YOSSARIAN

Yes, it will.

MAJOR MAJOR

I mean it, Yossarian. You'll have to keep on your toes every minute of every day. They'll bend heaven and earth to catch you.

YOSSARIAN

I'll keep on my toes.

MAJOR MAJOR

You'll have to jump.

YOSSARIAN

I'll jump.

[YOSSARIAN *exits through the doorway.* NATELY'S WHORE *moves behind him with the knife*]

MAJOR MAJOR

Jump!

[YOSSARIAN *jumps aside. The knife comes down, missing him by inches, and he runs off.* NATELY'S WHORE *chases out after him, brandishing the long knife*]

CHAPLAIN

Run, Yossarian! Run!

chaplain

[*To* MAJOR MAJOR, *after* YOSSARIAN *and* NATELY'S WHORE *have gone*]

Well, Major? What are you going to do?

[MAJOR MAJOR *thinks a moment. Then he puts on his fake mustache and large sunglasses, offers a friendly wave, and exits by way of the window. The* CHAPLAIN *starts away with an exuberant expression*]

My dear and darling beautiful wife. I have punched Colonel Cathcart in the nose. I await the consequences happily. They think I am crazy.

[*He exits with a smile*]

[*Curtain*]

PAGE. 13
104
184
192

2718   228